Praise for Restorying Your Story

In *Restorying Your Story,* Dr. Gauthier lays bare his own life experiences to introduce a model of healing through the Medicine Wheel Tipi model and Restorying Your Story process. In his work, Dr. Gauthier blends real world stories with academic evidence that offers a glimmer of hope in restorying many of the painful histories Indigenous people and communities have had to endure. Dr. Gauthier's work has the potential to impact the painful reality of overrepresentation of Indigenous people incarcerated in Canada, while offering industry and government a tool to improve on their efforts to increase their Indigenous cultural competencies through the incorporation of Dr. Gauthier's method into the required training of their personnel. For Indigenous communities, Dr. Gauthier's work offers a pathway to a new story that can empower and offer a true vision of self-determination for future generations.

   David Snowdon
   Federal Negotiation Manager
   Crown Indigenous Relations

This monograph offers profound insight into how we can heal from past trauma and learn to thrive—not in spite of it, but because of it. Just as importantly, it presents a pathway to healing and growth through Dr. Gauthier's own Indigenous lens, integrating lived experience and traditional knowledge.

This work is essential reading, particularly for non-Indigenous service providers who seek to support Indigenous communities. It not only deepens understanding but also challenges non-Indigenous individuals—whose ancestors played a role in the tragedies of colonialism and current colonial oppressions and structures—to recognize their unconscious biases and adopt a more culturally responsive and effective approach to support.

Ernie Hilton, MSc. CYCA

Executive Director

HomeBridge Youth Society

I was deeply moved by how Michael shared his own experiences, the impact of those events, and the unwavering belief that he deserved a better life... He chose to write this book so others may believe in their own ability to overcome, to know that they too deserve a better life. He reminds us that we are not defined by our past.

Reading this book is a sacred experience; its pages are filled with powerful stories of resilience, transformation, and hope. Neither Michael nor those who participate in the Restorying Your Story exercises shy away from the opportunity to share their stories in the hopes of living a better life.

I highly recommend this book to anyone interested in learning about the Restorying Your Story exercise and discovering how to move beyond negative past experiences toward healing and growth.

Grace Campbell, BEd

Program Manager

Policy and Indigenous Relations

———————————

Mike Gauthier's Restorying Your Story is a powerful tool to help anyone who is struggling with their past—or their past in their present—to find opportunity and fresh beginnings out of the smouldering ashes of trauma and hardship. Mike's courage to share his own story and the story of how he came to restorying adds depth, vulnerability, and authenticity to inspire our own courageous journey through this book and its methodology. It's easy to talk forever about a difficult past, but what Mike offers is a toolkit with clear instructions on how to overcome the monsters in our heads. He encourages and inspires his readers to take the plunge and turn stops into steps!

Heather Jill Scott, Ph.D.

Dr. Michael Gauthier's breakthrough book is a must-read for anyone who wants to better understand the traumatic effects on Indigenous people who have suffered child abuse, neglect, and incarceration in its various forms: residential schools, childcare system, youth detention centres, and prisons.

Based on his own life experiences, traditional Indigenous knowledge, the teachings of Elders, and his own research working with Indigenous men who have suffered abuse and incarceration, Dr. Michael Gauthier has developed an effective healing, rehabilitation, and restorative system that not only can be applied to Indigenous people who have experienced trauma, pain, and loss, but also anyone else, Indigenous and non-Indigenous, who desires healing and self-improvement.

This book contains a practical toolkit and how to help those who need understanding, healing, and a path to a happier, healthier, and rewarding life.

Stewart Guiboche

Legal Counsel, Department of Justice, Canada (retired)

Restorying Your Story

Reclaiming Your Voice
in the Face of Past Injustice

Dr. Michael Gauthier

Medicine Wheel Publishing

Medicine Wheel Publishing acknowledges that we live and work on the traditional and unceded lands of the Coast Salish People, including the T'Sou-ke People, the W̱SÁNEĆ People, Sc'ianew People, and the lək̓ʷəŋən Peoples.

Cover Design: Jeff Werner
Editor: Zoe Mix
Editor: Alicia Hibbert (Edified Projects)
Editorial Contributor: Matti McLeod
Proofreader: Patricia Robertson
All rights reserved.

ISBN 9781778540745

Published in 2025 by Medicine Wheel Publishing in Canada.
www.medicinewheelpublishing.com

Printed in PRC

10 9 8 7 6 5 4 3 2 1

Funded by the Government of Canada · Financé par le gouvernement du Canada · Canada

Sensitivity Warning

This book addresses sensitive topics including residential school, substance abuse, incarceration, and intergenerational trauma.These topics are addressed with the intention of helping readers create a healthier future for themselves and others. Please take care while reading this book.

Toll-Free Help Lines

24-hour National Indian Residential School Crisis Line
1-866-925-4419

Hope for Wellness Helpline
1-855-242-3310

Kids Help Phone
kidshelpphone.ca
1-800-668-6868

National Overdose Response Service (NORS)
www.nors.ca
1-888-688-6677

Suicide Crisis Helpline
988.ca
Call or text 988

Table of Contents

Acknowledgements

This book would not have been possible without the assistance, guidance, and wisdom of Dr. Sam McKegney and Dr. Jill Scott. Without my family's understanding, patience, and support, I would not be in a position to have written this book. Most of my balance and direction are from my beautiful wife, Carolyn. Both of my children, Sydney and Payton, have shown me how intergenerational trauma can be changed. I also want to thank my business partner and friend, Mark Ethier, for being a mentor and providing me with some good life teachings. In addition, I want to thank all of the Indigenous people who I worked with over the years and who have been my role models in terms of resiliency, staying strong, and overcoming past trauma.

Foreword

> " *From around the kitchen tables of the people I have*
> *known have come stories of the heart. Great trust and*
> *love were required to enable the bearer to part with the*
> *tale. If I wrote for a lifetime I could never re-tell all the*
> *stories that people have given me. I am not sure what to*
> *do with that, except that I shall try to grasp the essence*
> *of our lives and to help weave a new story. A story in*
> *which pain is not our way of life.*"
> — Lee Maracle, *I Am Woman: A Native Perspective*
>   *on Sociology and Feminism* (Page 6)

Stories are shared in all kinds of places—in coffee shops and classrooms, in theatres and on buses, in locker rooms and pubs and counsellors' offices, in homes around kitchen tables (as the great Stó:lō writer Lee Maracle reminds us above), within the pages of books like this one, and within our minds and hearts as we revisit our memories. The types of stories we tell and the details upon which we focus are informed by the context of their telling. Where we are and whom we're with condition what we share, what we reconfigure, and what we keep to ourselves.

The Restorying Your Story method illuminates pathways to personal growth and healing through a process of remembering, reckoning with, and reclaiming power over your past. In contexts where people have been fragmented by past experiences—or *dis*-membered—*re*-membering can prove a powerful process of reclamation. As Michael Gauthier writes in *Restorying Your Story*, "when someone asks a person to remember, they are also asking them to create." Such deeply personal work is made possible by conditions of safety and support, conditions in which participants can be vulnerable and imaginative. In the restorying circles Gauthier conducted with formerly incarcerated Indigenous men at Four Directions Aboriginal Students' Centre (4D) in Kingston/Katarokwi, the participants' shared commitment to support, reciprocity, and mutual accountability created the conditions in which "Powerful words," as Michael writes, could be "gifted to the circle with sensitivity and received gratefully by its members." Listening in that space was every bit as generative as speaking; each member's care for the stories of others enabled the collectivity to grow strong.

I was honoured to act as a witness at each of these weekly restorying sessions when I was Mike's PhD supervisor, just as I'm honoured to have been asked to write the foreword for the present volume. How the men's stories interacted with each other back in 2016 reminded me of what Kānaka Maoli scholar Ty P. Kāwiki Tengan calls "Talk story," which creates a "sense of shared identity because you're having and engaging in this communicative event, this modelling of personal stories after collective stories. Making these emotional, personal, and collective connections, that's what solidifies a sense of community."[1] Gauthier's restorying circles allowed the men to pick up threads from each other's stories, entwine them with story threads of their own, and thereby weave themselves garments of warmth and protection in which the hard work of reinvigorating identity would be possible.

The Anishinaabe writer Gerald Vizenor tells us, "You can't understand the world without telling a story. There isn't any center to the world but a story."[2] However, the dominant stories that circulate on Turtle Island are often corrosive. The settler colonial project has been one of dispossession—the removal of Indigenous bodies, communities, and nations from sacred lands in order to speed resource extraction, white settlement, and the naturalization of the Canadian nation state. It has involved the attempted obliteration of Indigenous nations as political entities and the attempted disappearing of Indigenous Peoples through indoctrination, incarceration, and death. And yet dominant narratives tend to treat these genocidal histories as inevitabilities rather than as crimes with perpetrators and beneficiaries. The stories we often hear in the media, on television, in film, and in literature are often

---

1   McKegney, S (Ed). (2014). *Masculindians: Conversations about Indigenous manhood.* University of Manitoba Press. P. 118
2   Vizenor, Gerald. (1990, 1991.) *Gerald Vizenor: The Trickster Heirs of Columbus.* An interview with Laura Coltelli. In: Laura Coltelli, ed. Native American Literature, Forum 2, 3.

those that absolve the nation state and ease the culpability of white settler Canadians like me. According to Cherokee Nation scholar Daniel Heath Justice, "the most corrosive of all is the story of *Indigenous deficiency*."[3] The Indigenous men with whom Mike worked at 4D had inherited this story throughout their lives. It was so pervasive that they almost never contextualized their experience in relation to "racism," "colonialism," or "oppression," tending rather to register fault first within themselves. Justice argues that "the most wounding way in which this story of Indigenous deficiency works is in how it displaces our other stories, the stories of complexity, hope, and possibility."[4] The restorying process enabled these resilient Indigenous men not only to find more nurturing stories than those they had inherited from the oppressive society around them but to take ownership of those stories and craft them into a vision of future well-being and empowerment.

What you hold in your hands is a gift—a gift created when Michael Gauthier braided his experiential, critical, and cultural knowledge into medicine to keep his own life in balance in the shadow of childhood trauma and to offer hope and healing for others. Emerging from Gauthier's own life journey through the restorying process, developed and piloted

3   Justice, Daniel Heath. *Why Indigenous Literatures Matter*. Wilfrid Laurier University Press, 2018.

4   McKegney, Sam, Ed. *Masculindians: Stories about Indigenous Manhood*. University of Manitoba Press, 2014.

within his multi-year doctoral study at Queen's University, and then honed through multiple restorying sessions with Life-Circle Consulting, *Restorying Your Story* combines ancient wisdom with practical, everyday knowledge, personal narratives with broader political commentary, and historical and critical context with useful tools to help readers take control of their lives and their stories. There is a section in *Restorying Your Story* called "Persistence of Hope." This book—like the stories of its author and of restorying circle participants found within—shows us how hope can be kept alive in the flesh, in the heart, in gestures, expressions, and words even in the darkest of times, and how, like embers, hope can be stoked back to flame through story, flame that gives ever more light and heat when fed by the stories of others in community.

Sam McKegney
Kingston/Katarokwi
3 April 2025

Restorying Trauma:
A Journey to Healing

There was once an eagle soaring high in the sky, carrying the prayers of the Indigenous people to the Creator. But one day, hunters shot him down, wounding his wing and sending him crashing to the ground. Unable to fly, the eagle lay helpless until a local settler farmer found him. The farmer took the injured eagle back to his farm, placing him in a chicken pen among the other chickens.

The farmer tended to the eagle's wounded wing and told him, "You can leave anytime—you don't belong here in a chicken coop." But as time passed, the eagle, surrounded by chickens, began to forget his true identity. He watched the chickens pecking at the dirt, and though he did not feel like one of them, he eventually gave in to his surroundings. He began to behave like a chicken, scratching the earth and flapping weakly instead of soaring. He lost connection to his true nature, believing he was nothing more than a chicken.

One day, an Indigenous man came to the farm and asked the farmer for a drink of water. As the farmer went to fetch it, the Indigenous man looked into the chicken pen and was shocked to see an eagle among the chickens, pecking at the dirt like he had never flown before.

"I'll take that eagle off your hands," the Indigenous man told the farmer, "He doesn't belong there."

The farmer shrugged and said, "Take him. That's one less mouth to feed."

The Indigenous man carried the eagle under his arm, speaking to him gently. "You are a magnificent bird," he said. "You do not belong among the chickens. You were meant to soar."

He took the eagle to the highest mountain and told him, "You have gifts. You are powerful. You were born to fly high and carry the prayers of the people to the Creator. I'm going to throw you off here. You must remember who you are." Then, with great care, he threw the eagle off the mountain, expecting him to spread his wings and soar.

But the eagle did not fly. He crashed to the ground, once again pecking at the dirt like a chicken. The Indigenous man did not give up. He picked up the eagle and carried him back up the mountain, repeating his words of encouragement. Again, he threw the eagle into the sky, and again, the eagle fell.

Time and time again, the Indigenous man lifted the eagle, speaking to him with love and reminding him of his true nature. He told the eagle that he was meant to soar high into the sky, carrying the struggles and prayers of the Indigenous people to the Creator—the struggles of addiction, poverty, unemployment, and violence that weighed heavily on their communities.

He also told the eagle that everyone has gifts, and it is only when we believe in ourselves that we can find them and use them. Then, something miraculous happened. The eagle finally believed the words of the Indigenous man. He spread his wings, caught the wind, and soared high into the sky, reclaiming his true identity.

In this story, the eagle serves as an analogy for a person who has been negatively impacted by their past trauma, robbed of their identity, and made choices that led to them being incarcerated inside a prison (the "chicken coop"). When they go to prison, they become further separated from their identity by taking on a prisoner persona simply to survive.

Over time, the prisoner becomes a chicken and loses all sense of their culture, language, family, and community connection. They become someone else, no longer someone with a sense of cultural pride, cultural connection, or family unity, which is what is needed for them to become an eagle.

Although the eagle is picked up by an Indigenous person and removed from the chicken pen, and the Indigenous person tries to get the eagle to fly, the eagle believes they are still a chicken and does not recognize their ability to fly. They forget they are an eagle and can fly, so they continue to peck away and act like a chicken.

Similarly, many inmates who are released from prison continue to behave like chickens, never believing in their own abilities. They forget that each and every one of them has gifts and special skills, like the eagle. They continue to behave like chickens and this leads them back to the chicken coop.

This eagle story was shared by Linda Zaluska, the Elder who helped facilitate a few of the restorying circles for my PhD project. The story was offered to help the PhD research participants believe in themselves and to recognize the many gifts that they all possess as Indigenous men. As a child, everyone has gifts: love, kindness, caring, respect, and courage. These gifts can be lost when we forget who we are—and getting lost in the criminal justice system can obscure our identities.

By becoming trapped within the chicken coop of incarceration—from residential schools to foster care to group homes to young offenders' facilities to the prison system—many Indigenous people have experienced the suppression of their identities. Just like the eagle, so many Indigenous people have lost their identity due to historical mistreatment and damage caused by factors such as residential schools, the child welfare system, and intergenerational trauma.

However, the eagle and Indigenous people will soar because of their innate resilience and ability to survive amid adversity and past trauma. Indigenous people can reclaim their identities and rediscover their gifts and potential to become who they want to be with a belief in their culture and teachings. Indigenous culture and spirituality benefit the Indigenous person by identifying strengths within one's core identity.

Privilege and choice are directly correlated with a person's wealth and opportunities, and this affects non-Indigenous people too. More wealth and opportunities lead to better education and the chance to meet people who have connections and positive support. This privilege negates the necessity to make decisions out of desperation or trauma and allows that person the opportunity to make healthier choices.

A lack of privilege and choices, on the other hand, can cause people to become disconnected from their families and communities, leading many down a road of poverty with lack of education and employment leading to negative choices, and then down a path of criminality. Many individuals who have no connection to their family or community, let alone to themselves, struggle with low self-worth and tend to be embarrassed about their situation, shying away from being noticed. So, the typical behaviour is to keep their head down, out of sight and out of mind, pecking in the dirt and continuing the behaviours of a chicken, which leads to bad choices and negative consequences.

I hope that restorying can have a positive effect on individuals in Canada who suffer from trauma, by helping them break free from the negativity of the past. Through restorying, they hopefully will get a better sense of balance and find who they are and where they want to go in their healing journey.

Restorying for me started when I quit drinking at the age of twenty-two years old. I knew I deserved better and this gave me a second chance to do better with my life.

I spoke with a psychologist who referred to the "Little Mike" inside me, the part of me who had experienced all the harmful stuff that happened to me growing up. Little Mike tended to recreate those past traumas, causing me, as "Big Mike," to continue to relive them over and over and over again. I was asked, "At what point do you decide to stop reliving the past trauma?"

I answered this question when I was around thirty-eight years old, starting to behave in a healthier way by restorying my story. Little Mike had ruled the roost too long, and it was time for Big Mike to take over and stop Little Mike from turning up the volume on "stinking thinking"!

I have been through quite a bit of trauma as a child. I believe that this trauma has led me on a journey where things were meant to happen. It was no mistake that I ended up helping and working with individuals stuck in the criminal justice system. It was no mistake that I completed my master's degree in education and my PhD in cultural studies, looking at how our past trauma can impact us in so many ways. Most importantly, it was no mistake that this led to Life-Circle.ca, where we get people to share their stories and then restory them. Over the last fifteen-plus years, I have been restorying my own story and am happy to share this process in this book.

Growing up for me could be described as sad and chaotic. I grew up in a very dysfunctional home with violence and alcoholism. I never really witnessed any form of healthy parenting, even though I had three sets of parents—biological, foster, and adoptive parents.

As a youth, I defended and took care of myself, and looked out for my younger siblings. It was not an enjoyable time, but I survived it. I lived on Parliament Street in downtown Toronto—at the time, it was called "Cabbagetown" and was one of the poorest areas in Toronto. I never went anywhere outside of my neighbourhood. The only time I left was when I was picked up and we moved to PEI (Prince Edward Island) with my biological father. After living in PEI for about one year, I was adopted and moved to Germany with my adoptive parents. I lived in Germany for five years, moved to New Brunswick, and then my adoptive parents settled back in PEI.

I loved to play sports, especially soccer and hockey. I also enjoyed the game of Ping-Pong at the local YMCA, because it was free. Unfortunately, I was not really interested in subjects at school, but I did love going to school as it was an escape from my family home, where there was misery. I never did miss one minute of class and made sure I just passed my classes, as most times I was either tired due to my alcoholic adoptive mother keeping us up all night or hungry as we did not have much food to eat.

Despite these challenges growing up, my lightbulb moment happened when I was working inside the prison system and saw so many individuals continue to live their lives in the same way they had been for years, which were inflicted and infected by colonialism and its destructive past. I, too, realized that my life was inflicted and infected, and many times I would think about the past, letting myself relive the trauma in my present life. I realized there must be a better way to help myself and others; that I could help others manage their past trauma in a good way.

This is why the Medicine Wheel Tipi model (which I will expand on in the next chapter) and the Restorying Your Story process were created. It was created to help people get a sense of balance, have a good way to live today *for* today, and not get stuck in the past.

In the early 2000s, I decided to pursue a second degree, which I earned in Native Studies from Laurentian University, where I made the honour roll. I then utilized those achievements and applied for the Master of Education program at Queen's University in 2008, graduating in 2011. I never imagined I would pursue a PhD, but during this time, I was introduced to Professor Sam McKegney. We developed a strong working relationship, and he agreed to supervise me. I pursued my PhD and wrote my dissertation on restorying with previously incarcerated Indigenous men. I graduated in 2017 from Queen's University. Throughout this journey, I worked full-time in the prison system while staying involved with my children's activities and life by coaching both hockey and soccer.

Another catalyst for creating the Restorying Your Story process with the Medicine Wheel Tipi model was when I witnessed so many residential school survivors at the final Truth and Reconciliation event in Ottawa in June 2015 retell their past traumatic stories, continuing to bring up and punish themselves by retelling them. Organizers provided support through a 1-800 hotline. I felt that more could be done than to have the survivors who were experiencing harmful thoughts telephone a counsellor they don't know. Something else was missing, which is part of my journey to create the Restorying Your Story healing process.

Richard Wagamese wrote that we are the stories we tell ourselves.[5] How do we change these stories that seem to own and direct us? How can individuals externalize their traumas and see that they can write their story in a different way, leading to different outcomes instead of continuing the legacy of intergenerational trauma? A person who continues to live a difficult story must be willing and able to change that challenging story into a healthier one. Without the desire to change, nothing will change. I also believe that a person needs a community or organizations such as Narcotics Anonymous (NA) and Alcoholics Anonymous (AA) to support them to make that change. It is easy to tell a person, "This is what you need to do to change the story of the past," but it is very difficult to actually make and sustain changes to overcome the past trauma and move onto a healthier present. It has to come from inside. People can have the choice to look back on their story and say to themselves, "What did I learn from that situation to make me better for today?" or they can say to themselves, "I am an idiot, I don't deserve anything in life, and I will continue to live in a bad way as I am a victim of my past." The choice is theirs!

---

5   Wagamese, 2017, para. 1

I define restorying as a practice of changing one's eyes to see the past differently and hopefully to create a vision of a healthy future. I first explored this in my PhD project, where I wanted to create a space for Indigenous males in an urban setting who were involved with the criminal justice system, a position I, too, had found myself in years ago. I wanted them to be able to share stories and learn to restory in a supportive setting.

The first restorying circle I held went better than I expected. It was held at the Four Directions Indigenous Student Centre at Queen's University, Kingston. The room was in the front of the building, and the building was from the mid-fifties to sixties—it had a very homey sense about it. It was weathered on the outside, but the room had a good sense of energy and cultural items that made you feel like you belonged in an Indigenous space of sharing and healing.

It was a Monday night, and I was not sure if my fellow participants were going to show up. But they did, and we had a great opening prayer by the Elder, who set the tone for the rest of the night. He made everyone feel comfortable and welcomed, which allowed all the participants to feel safe, knowing that if they shared their stories, it would be kept confidential and respected.

I felt a bit nervous at first because I was not sure which way the evening would go. It could either be a success or a complete failure. A lot was riding on the circle being successful as it was a huge part of getting my PhD degree. I have sat in a lot of healing and talking circles, so I was used to hearing people's stories. However, this time, I was like the circle conductor and was implementing a new model, asking people to share their stories, starting with their childhood and on to their adult years. I wanted to see how effective my model would be received, but more importantly how it would help people open up about their stories and past trauma. Any time you hear someone share traumatic stories, it can impact you and emotionally drain you, and this first circle was no exception. However, it can also create a safe place for that person to release some of the negativity they have been carrying around with them for years. It was rewarding for me to listen to them share and release the ghosts from their closet. Since then, I believe we have led close to thirty restorying circles.

I experienced the impacts of residential schooling, the child welfare system, and intergenerational trauma within my family. My biological mother was a residential school survivor who was exposed to a volatile environment that robbed her of a healthy lifestyle. Her trauma led to the fragmentation of my family and my placement in several foster homes before eventually being adopted into another dysfunctional family. Growing up in this environment and being exposed to violence, alcoholism, and abuse informed my own troubles with the law.

After spending time reflecting on, revising, and restorying my personal history, I have been able to rise above intergenerational trauma. The vision for my PhD project and consulting work emerged by braiding together my experiences as an Indigenous man working within Corrections with my experiences confronting the Canadian legal system as a youth and with academic understandings gained during my studies in Sociology, Native Studies, Education, and Cultural Studies.

I have spent time reflecting, revising, and restorying my own life history, and this has helped form my healing journey. I have participated in and facilitated sharing circles conducted by Elders within the prison system and in Indigenous communities. These circles formed the groundwork for my research and subsequent projects. I found that there were few culturally relevant programs available outside prison for individuals impacted by past trauma, especially ones that utilized a model like the one we use: a Medicine Wheel Tipi. My goal is to continue to create such forums in which restorying will be facilitated as a strategy to support individuals coming from all backgrounds.

The Restorying Your Story method was developed over many years of working with Indigenous people who were incarcerated and caught within the jaws of the criminal justice system (CJS). I have witnessed individuals who continued to let the past trauma haunt them in their current lives and constantly relive that negative past life. This leads them down a similar path to being trapped within the criminal justice system. The actual term *restorying* came from my discussion with one of my PhD supervisors at Queen's University, where she talked about being able to speak a different, healthier story in one's own mind.

Since 2017, Life-Circle Consulting, a business I co-founded, has expanded to facilitate restorying circles across many types of organizations so that folks can, in the words of one participant, start "living for the present and future" and "reinforce the path forward." We facilitate restorying circles for Indigenous and non-Indigenous people who have been impacted and stuck in their past trauma. These circles give them an opportunity to share, listen, and restory their story in a supportive setting. As another participant at a session in 2023 said, they are about "the importance of addressing one's past to better prepare for the future and re-establish connections to life." While I started working with incarcerated people, restorying works for anyone, and we've worked with many organizations since. Some examples from these sessions will be shared throughout the chapters of this book.

What is Restorying?

Restorying is an Indigenous-based counselling method. It uses the Medicine Wheel Tipi (MWT) model, which I developed and is derived from my life experiences and studies. This method aims to help Indigenous people by providing a vehicle to create a healthy path forward for their lives using traditional concepts and beliefs. The method includes tools and research that help me create an environment that is safe and culturally relevant. Restorying circles can last anywhere from one to three hours per circle, depending on how much participants open up about their past trauma. There are not many rules, other than showing respect for the circle. Participants take turns speaking, moving either clockwise or counterclockwise, depending on the cultural practices of the Indigenous community we're working with. The facilitators are there to guide and respond to the participants, offering support if they are stuck or are struggling with opening up and sharing their stories.

Every restorying circle begins with an Elder opening the session. We start by explaining the purpose behind restorying one's story. Then, we do a few exercises, including icebreakers, to help participants feel comfortable and ready to share their own stories. We also provide examples of other people's stories to give them an idea of what they are invited to share. Once a safe environment and trust are established, the journey begins toward a healthier perspective and life.

For the restorying process, we have a few questions that act as a guide to help the participants think about their past stories. But it's important to remember that the adaptation of a new perspective is individually specific and varies—each person moves at their own pace. The key to the most transformative restorying circles is when participants are willing to fully open up and share the trauma they've been carrying for a long time. Big shifts happen when they are vulnerable. At the end of the session, we do a check-in to make sure everyone is in a good place. An Elder closes the circle, and they're available afterward for anyone who needs extra support or would like to talk about their feelings. Each step in this process is about building a healthier foundation where we can collectively acknowledge and remove the pain of the past and the realities of today as obstacles limiting future progress.

Healing can often be aided by the opportunity to share one's life story with calmness when before it was interrupted by chaos and painful emotions.

There was a restorying circle we held in Wikwemikong First Nation that has always stood out for me. It occurred at Rainbow Lodge treatment facility. I remember that there were more than twenty participants, mostly women, who were all workers at the lodge. The first couple of participants were hesitant to share their stories. Then, suddenly, a young woman who gave herself the nickname "Awesome Julie" shared her story. It was not only powerful but gut-wrenching to hear of all the trauma that she endured as a child and young adult. But what made the moment so incredible was that, because she was so courageous to open up about her story, the others after her also opened up. So, "Awesome Julie" unleashed the floodgates, giving others the bravery to talk about their past struggles. I told her that her nickname was given to her for a reason. She *is* "Awesome Julie" because she had the strength to share, inspiring others, after overcoming all of her past traumas.

For many, the first step to combat past traumas is to expose long-buried experiences and feelings. Sharing these stories reveals and exposes what people have hidden, giving voice to what others have silenced.[6] Restorying is also a dynamic form of storytelling that revisits in order to restore.[7] Restorying engages Indigenous people to reclaim their voices. It helps them piece together a broken and silenced past. In doing so, it transforms stories of victimhood into stories of resilience. Restorying does not change the bad things that happened but allows one to look at those areas and move forward. Restorying also means creating spaces where Indigenous peoples can take back their voices and begin to rebuild identities that have been fragmented by colonial

6   McKegney, 2007, p. 5
7   Voyageur, Brearley & Calliou, 2014, p. 4

oppression—fragmentation that has been sustained, even made worse, by substance abuse.

According to Meseyton,[8] the healing journey typically involves identifying areas of change, telling one's story with space for a new Indigenous identity to emerge, analyzing the trauma and links to unhealthy behaviour, and creating a new vision of self where individual healing is part of community healing.[9] When someone asks a person to remember, they are also asking them to create. Remembering is a creative process that happens in a space where storytelling is encouraged. The person remembering chooses which parts of their history to share and how to share them. My PhD research participants, and all participants in sessions since, had control over the stories they chose to tell about themselves and their histories. They aren't just victims of their histories, but rather, they are empowered to a certain degree to understand those histories in ways that work for them. They are creative agents and not just passive victims.

Throughout the restorying process, it's important to make sure that participants engage with their histories. Tousignant said that restorying often requires multiple retellings to allow individuals to create new understandings of their identities.[10] Many have suffered, endured, and demonstrated the true

---

8   Meseyton, 2005.
9   Meseyton, 2005, p. 212.
10 Tousignant, 2009.

meaning of resilience by surviving their past traumatic events. They bring this strength to the restorying circles as well as their compassion and support for the other participants. As such, the restorying process is repeatedly affirmed to be strengths-based. Everyone has a story, and these stories can be changed; no one story sums us up. At each restorying circle, participants are invited to share their personal stories with the group. For my PhD research, every session covered a different stage of the participants' life journey. It started with childhood, then their teenage years, adulthood, and future goals, including their elder years.

For restorying circles that I lead, the presence of Indigenous Elders or advisors facilitates a focus on healing and growth. Elders have shared that although participants have painful memories, they can clear the air through a smudge, prayer, and ceremony. Restorying circles don't focus on the pain, suffering, abuse, addictions, or experiences but rather on remembering the child within who has been isolated and forgotten. These circles allow each participant to catch glimpses of themselves and what they may become in the future. For participants who have long struggled in isolation, the restorying circles allow for a space to learn to connect with others. Restorying circles enable people to look within themselves to see where they are out of balance and identify what they need to do to regain balance. This is a way of shedding light on the ghosts in the closet.

Wheel of Incarceration

The Wheel of Incarceration was the first model I created on my journey toward creating the Medicine Wheel Tipi model and restorying circles. The wheel of incarceration shows how past trauma impacts people's lives, which can lead to them getting caught within the criminal justice system. By becoming trapped within the chicken coop of incarceration—from residential schools to foster care to group homes to young offenders' facilities to the prison system—Indigenous people have experienced the suppression of their identities.

Many Indigenous adult inmates have graduated from young offenders' facilities to federal prisons. As children, some of these individuals were removed from their families and placed into residential schools or apprehended by the child welfare authorities and placed into foster homes or adopted outside their community. This means that from a very young age their lives had been (re)organized by the coercive power of Canadian law. Such involvement with the justice system accelerates from youth to adolescence to adulthood. It can start out as probation. Then it might go into days or weeks at a group home. Next, it could continue into months and perhaps years at a young offenders' facility. After that, it might evolve into years at a provincial jail and then a federal penitentiary. Indigenous inmates become institutionalized through their encounters with the criminal justice system and, as a result, become further disconnected from their individual, familial, and cultural identities.

The wheel of incarceration reveals a cycle of oppression and disconnection arising from systemic trauma. After developing this model, I knew that I needed to find a tool that was more strengths-based. This is what led me to the next iteration: the healing and restorative power of the Medicine Wheel Tipi model, rooted in Indigenous teachings and practices.

The Tipi and Medicine Wheel

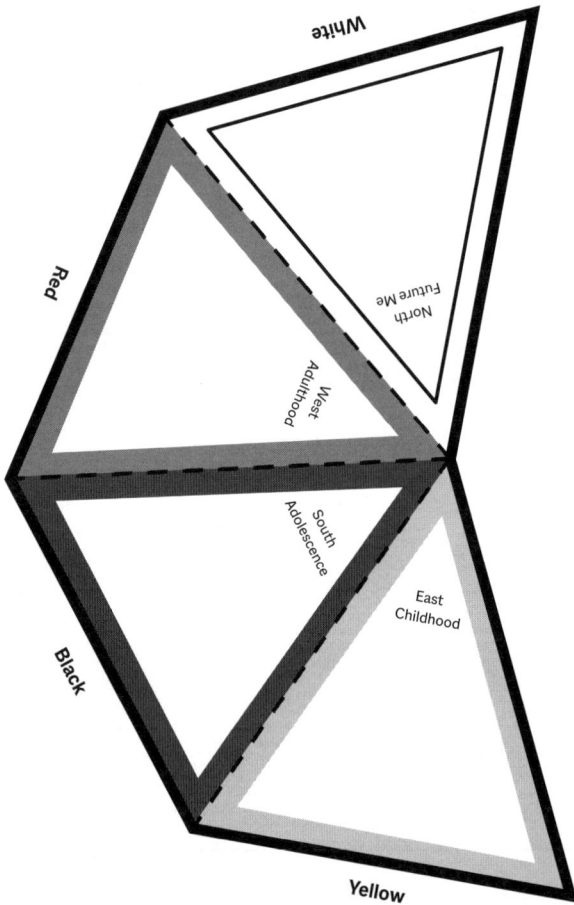

White

Red

North
Future Me

West
Adulthood

South
Adolescence

East
Childhood

Black

Yellow

One day, when I was doing my PhD at Queen's University, it just dawned on me to combine both the Medicine Wheel and tipi together to create a healing *model*, but more importantly, a healing *process* to help people restore their story.

The Medicine Wheel teachings and the tipi are culturally recognizable by most Indigenous People across Canada. The Medicine Wheel has been used in Indigenous historical written and oral knowledge for centuries, representing many First Nations worldviews. It represents a holistic way of healing. The Medicine Wheel Tipi model was created through my work in the Indigenous department of Correctional Service Canada, as well as my experiences working with Elders and Indigenous people that I try to help reintegrate back into the community.

One of the main reasons for choosing the Medicine Wheel was to help participants who felt imbalanced. The Medicine Wheel helps restore this imbalance by looking at and utilizing the four aspects of a person's well-being: physical, mental, emotional, and spiritual.

The tipi aspect of the model was chosen because, traditionally, the tipi was a place where people gathered to share their stories. These storytelling sessions traditionally took place among several Indigenous cultures, including the Cree, Blackfoot, and Dakota. It's also a recognizable structure across Canada, meaning many Indigenous and non-Indigenous people could recognize what the structure of the tipi is and represents. For me, the tipi represents a safe place for individuals to come and share their stories and feel good about opening up. Also, the structure of a tipi is strong, which provides the opportunity for those who gather under it to open up and share their story.

The primary purpose of the Medicine Wheel Tipi method is for people to share their stories. During the circles, participants are given a double-sided copy of the Medicine Wheel Tipi model. For the first part of the Restorying Your Story process, we use this method to help people open up about their past, including the traumatic experiences they've been through.

We break this up into four life stages:

- East (0-7 years old): Early childhood
- South (7-18 years old): Teenage years—junior high and high school
- West (18-24 years old): Young adulthood
- North (present): Where they are in life now

Again, the first side of the Medicine Wheel Tipi model is for people to talk about their past trauma and this is usually the hardest part of the Restorying Your Story process—releasing painful memories, opening the closet, and letting the ghosts out. At the end of the workshop, each participant now has two tipis which they can continue to use in the future. They can continue to grow the second tipi with incremental healthy additives for their lives.

I should note that the somewhat pan-Indigenous character of the Medicine Wheel Tipi could be altered to make other more tribally specific models in future restorying circles. The Medicine Wheel Tipi model could be transformed into another cultural symbolic model or teaching application, where it would serve the needs of a particular Indigenous community. If one were conducting restorying circles in Iqaluit, an Inukshuk might provide a more useful cultural symbol to provoke reflection than a tipi. Or if one were conducting a circle among entirely Haudenosaunee men, then a Medicine Longhouse might be better.

The same goes for other cultures. Even among non-Indigenous participants, the concept of the Medicine Wheel Tipi resonates. This is because everyone, Indigenous and non-Indigenous people alike, has their own unique weaknesses and strengths. Visualizing through a symbolic art form like the MWT can create new ways of thinking about one's history, opening up avenues to restorying.

The next part, which takes place either the next day or in a later session, is focused on having the individuals revisit, reframe, and retell their stories in a healthier way. Again, we get the participants to look at their stories related to their childhood, their teenage years, their young adult years, and their current life. This is also not an easy process for people to look at their past traumatic stories and be able to tell a healthier story. It just doesn't happen that way. To help, we give them examples of other people's stories and how they restoried them. I also share my story and talk about how I've reframed it.

Everyone who uses the MWT model will see things slightly differently. This difference is because everyone has their own unique gifts that are needed to serve themselves and others. When we use the Medicine Wheel Tipi as a framework we see our weaknesses and our strengths. One must visualize oneself in the middle of the Medicine Wheel, connected to all points.

The East is the place of new beginnings. All of us will return to this place as we experience new things in our lives. Everyone has a place in life's journey, and we need to recognize what we are meant to do in this journey to grow as people.

The most difficult and valuable gift of **the South** is to express one's feelings openly and freely without hurting others.

The gift of prayer occurs in **the West**. This allows us to be spiritually connected. People need to find room in their lives for prayer, to reflect on their own creation and what they are to do with their lives. The greatest lesson of the West is to accept ourselves for who we are. As human beings, we develop and grow in relation to our decisions, good and bad. Many people imagine themselves to have far less potential than they do.

The North is the winter, white as snow, like the white hair of our Elders. Not all gifts come easy and gaining the wisdom of age takes hard work and patience. To be a whole person, according to the teachings of the Medicine Wheel, is to be alive in a physical, emotional, mental, and spiritual way.

The MWT and Restorying Your Story methods start a journey to overcome the pain of the past and present cycles in our lives. Acknowledging that we all start with a pure, clean slate, which is later shaped by circumstances we can't always control, can help us see who we have become (Tipi 1).

Coming to terms with these moments of pain is important in creating a pathway forward. However, we need to make sure we don't dwell on them.

Instead, we should focus on who we want to be in a new, healthier direction (Tipi 2), knowing that we can write our new story. Some participants include important teachings from their cultures like the 7 Grandfather teachings or the Tipi Pole teachings to build a strong second tipi. Some include words of affirmation.

A good exercise to explore is to have a sheet with each person's name and pass it around for other participants to share positive affirmations. For example, Paul is caring, Brenda is a great singer, and Grant is very helpful. Then, each person will have a list of affirmations from the others to add to their own. Visualizing through a symbolic art form like the MWT can create new ways of thinking about one's own history, opening up avenues to restorying.

It is a culturally relevant and sensitive way to express their emotions. Using symbols can encourage a deeper and more unique reflection by participants. In this restorying approach, the creation of the MWT(s) allows the participants to create, see, and share their understandings of their gifts and identity.

One should not live in the past but learn from it. People suffering from past trauma may choose to deal with it by substance abuse, which may be the only way they know. For some, rather than face the pain for even one minute, they would rather mask it with drugs or alcohol. The MWT model encourages participants to reconnect with parts of themselves that have been damaged by trauma suffered as children and to connect with other participants through a process of restorying and mutual disclosure.

There is also a role for non-Indigenous allies that are willing to assist Indigenous people who have suffered past trauma caused by colonialism. For example, I have led restorying sessions with staff from social services organizations. It may be fair to say that those past non-Indigenous people who caused the tragic events of colonialism are now being replaced (restoried) with non-Indigenous people who want to help heal and make amends for all the wrongs of the past to help Indigenous people lead a healthier present and future.

Restorying the Lives of Indigenous People Connected with the Criminal Justice System

You might wonder what it is like for me, an Indigenous person, to work for the Government of Canada in criminal justice—and whether I have complicated feelings about it. One of the challenges for me is seeing so many people in the system who grew up just like I did. It really makes me realize what helped me break free and become a law-abiding citizen, while others continue to be trapped in the claws of the justice system. This is one of the more emotional aspects of my job. I want to do so much, but I have to step to the side and hope that maybe today is the day that a person decides to restory their story.

Colonization is very much connected to the criminal justice system. Historically, Indigenous Peoples dealt with crimes in their own traditional way. When First Nations people agreed to treaties and the *Indian Act* was created, as well as being controlled and assimilated by all the other Canadian government policies and legislations, their perspectives were not taken into account. The criminal justice system punished and put Indigenous people in jail for reasons like practising their culture, trying to leave their reserve, drinking alcohol, or trying to prevent the authorities from taking their children. These were all acts of deviance against the colonization of Indigenous Peoples, and the result was that Indigenous people were sent to prison because of the fact that they were just trying to protect their own religion, culture, families, and ways of living.

The over-representation of Indigenous people in the criminal justice system is the result of over a century of colonization that comes from a lack of access to employment, education, and privilege. Al Chartrand, President of the Native Clan Organization, once said: "[The Indigenous person] will probably appear before a white judge, be defended and prosecuted by white lawyers, and if he goes to jail, he'll be supervised by white guards. The justice system is often seen as a white man's weapon—a heavy hand that enforces his laws. It is them and us ... the white man's law."[11]

I designed the restorying circles for my PhD project to enable Indigenous men in Kingston, Ontario, whose lives had been impacted by the CJS, to engage in group discussions informed

---

11   York, 1990.

by Indigenous spiritual practices and attuned to the transformative power of stories. Traditional stories are one way that Indigenous Peoples honour the past, understand the present, and envision the future. Storytelling is a culturally appropriate way of mobilizing past experiences and forms of knowledge to confront new challenges and concerns. Sharing stories can validate the storytellers' experiences, taking authority away from non-Indigenous "experts" and investing authority in all members of the circle. The act of sharing stories can also offer others the strength, encouragement, and support they need to tell their own stories.[12]

The restorying that we did as part of my PhD project, developing and consciously evolving one's story, was designed to be a lengthy process. In this sense, it's quite distinct from a singular testimonial paradigm such as the one used in The Truth and Reconciliation Commission established under The Indian Residential Schools Settlement Agreement. One of the aims of restorying is to rediscover, to understand, and to gain interpretive agency over the past. We can rewrite past pains as battles won, not scars collected. We can outgrow the stories we've told ourselves. We can become something different. Perhaps we can even become the true selves that colonialism has sought to deny us.

My master's thesis research about the impact of residential schools, the child welfare system, and intergenerational

---

12   Brown & Strega, 2005, p. 252.

trauma on incarcerated Indigenous people highlighted those Indigenous inmates who had limited opportunities to examine their past negative stories leading to incarceration.[13] My PhD research extended this to build knowledge around restorying in a culturally relevant way with Indigenous ex-offenders in an urban setting.[14] It's important for me to share this research first because these experiences and knowledge frame our present scope of work at Life-Circle Consulting, where we facilitate and work with people who support individuals on their healing journeys.

My PhD project was also facilitated by my certifications in Aboriginal perception, cultural competency, reality therapy, control theory, and the "Coming Full Circle" training program, as well as by my participation in and facilitation of sharing circles conducted by Elders within the prison system and in Indigenous communities, some of which are ongoing. Anishinaabe writer Kateri Akiwenzie-Damm notes that "[a] lot of Indigenous men have learned what it means to be an Indigenous man from the worst possible sources, like residential school or child welfare system or jail, or parents who went through one or more of those systems and lacked the parenting skills that they needed in order to guide their sons."[15]

---

13   Gauthier, 2010.
14   Gauthier, 2017.
15   McKegney, 2014, p. 182.

Ironically, the programs that connect many Indigenous inmates to their cultures within prison settings are often unavailable to them upon release, particularly if they don't return to a reserve-based setting. For Indigenous former inmates who reside in an urban space like Kingston, Ontario—a small Canadian city of 125,000 people with a small but vibrant Indigenous population, multiple prisons, and limited cultural resources—the lack of opportunity to engage with personal and cultural histories may adversely impact healing and may indeed contribute to recidivism.

My PhD work had three interconnected objectives: first, to enable Indigenous people involved with the criminal justice system to improve their lives; second, to create greater awareness of colonial impediments to justice for Indigenous people by fostering counternarratives to the prevailing political rhetoric that we need 'more jails' in Canada to lock up the 'bad guys'; and third, to create new culturally safe models for politically engaged healing.

Four male Indigenous participants attended six restorying circles. Their ages ranged from late thirties to early fifties. Three of the participants were First Nations, and the fourth was Inuk. All the participants had participated in previous cultural activities like talking circles. They had all experienced incarceration within a federal institution. Three of the participants had resided in young offenders' facilities, such as a group home, open custody facility, or secure custody facility. Everyone in the group had served periods of incarceration in a provincial jail, had served multiple terms of incarceration, and at the time of the circles they were living in the community. Two of the group were employed full-time. During these restorying circles, all participants were supervised by the CJS and had certain conditions to follow.

In my PhD project, I recorded the experiences, views, and stories shared by Indigenous participants to shed new light on the conditions of power that inform their experiences and to create opportunities to restory their histories, fostering growth and healing. The restorying circles designed for my PhD project placed Indigenous men impacted by the CJS in dialogue with other Indigenous men who had endured similar experiences. These restorying circles were created to serve the needs of Indigenous former inmates with varying levels of traditional knowledge, spiritual connection, and cultural experience.

At the time that the Indigenous men agreed to participate in the restorying circles for my PhD project, each had already taken steps along his healing journey, many having found Elders, spiritual ceremonies, and healing circles to help them begin to bring forth and affirm their identities. Although the men all shared stories about being lost and isolated—one participant, for example, described that "inside" his younger self was "a little boy who had to be loved and cherished, because he was lonely"—they had begun to find their healing paths and an opportunity to share and hear different healthier

stories. Our circles provided a safe and supportive environment where they could speak to their earlier experiences,
gain insights from each other, and identify the strengths
that would continue to sustain them on pathways toward
well-being and empowerment.

On the first day of our restorying circles with incarcerated men in 2016, I introduced the men to the Medicine
Wheel Tipi and indicated how it would be used to help
them with their reflections. In this meeting, I told them that
the keywords and phrases on the wheel were taken from
my own experience and some of the difficult experiences
of Indigenous men I had dealt with in the prison system
throughout the previous two decades. I then indicated that,
in each subsequent meeting, I would focus on a particular
side of the Medicine Wheel Tipi that aligned with the subject
matter of that day's discussion—whether that was childhood,
adolescence, adulthood, or the future. When the men shared
their stories each day, I invited them to use the MWT as a
prompt if they so desired. However, I stressed that this was
entirely optional and that they didn't have to use the MWT
if they didn't want to.

The second restorying circle discussed the participants'
childhood stories. The third circle discussed the participants'
teen and young adult years. The fourth circle discussed
their adult experiences and stories. In the fifth circle, the
participants reflected on and discussed some of the previous
narratives to uncover strengths within themselves that
those stories display. They were also encouraged here to

think about the next steps and pathways forward in their healing journeys.

During the final circle, participants shared their thoughts on the restorying/reflecting/revisioning process regarding the project's goals of sharing with others, healing from past difficulties, and moving toward empowerment, balance, and personal and collective well-being. They were thanked for participating and contributing to this research study. The participants were given a framed graduation diploma from the restorying circles and a gift card to thank them for their generosity in sharing.

The participants were allowed to show up to and leave the circles at any time. No requirement was placed upon these individuals to share their stories. As we went around the circle at each session, the men were informed that they could share, pass, or leave the circle if they felt uncomfortable about any topic of discussion. Those who decided to participate in the research element of the project were invited to record their stories during the restorying process, but this was also voluntary. Tellingly, all participants agreed to have their stories recorded and incorporated into the findings of this study.

The criminal justice system has long failed Indigenous Peoples in Canada.[16] Statistics continue to show the over-representation of Indigenous people in all areas of the CJS.

---

16 RCAP, 1996; York, 1990.

In 2010/11, Indigenous people represented just over 3% of the Canadian population but represented roughly 27% of admissions to provincial prisons and 20% to federal prisons.[17] My hypothesis entering my PhD project—built from my experiences as a Cree scholar who had worked in the CJS for 21 years and had studied colonialism, intergenerational trauma, and carceral spaces (jails, young offender secure custody, and group home settings) like the residential school and child welfare system—was that restorying circles for Indigenous people involved with the CJS would offer a chance to contextualize their experiences with an unjust colonial history, deconstruct negative personal narratives, and enable healing to begin (or continue).

And this did come about. Remembering, sharing stories, and revitalizing our consciousness in a safe and culturally engaged sharing circle with the support of Elders and other Indigenous men enabled participants to reframe and restory their own histories in healthier, more generative ways.

---

17 Dauvergne, 2012, p. 11.

The Importance of Storytelling

" I understand the reason for the groups, I understand why they're put together, and they get the circles going because guys need it. Maybe I need it in a way at times, get me thinking again about things. Maybe get me talking about things I don't talk about enough. It's good to come someplace where you can share your childhood, you can share your story, share ideals. But most of all, it's good just to come at times. Meegwetch."
— Workshop Participant

I remember listening to Phyllis Webstad share her story about her experience of having her orange t-shirt taken from her at residential school. I remember listening to her share the trauma behind them removing that piece of clothing from her. I thought to myself that it would be powerful, if I had an opportunity like Phyllis, to author a book. At the end of her presentation, Phyllis indicated to the audience that her books are published by Medicine Wheel Publishing, now the publisher of this book.

Many Indigenous cultural practices, like storytelling, have been broken apart by decades of forced assimilation in residential schools and elsewhere. As shown in many historical records and survivor testimonies, students in residential schools were punished, often violently, for speaking their language and sharing their stories. Yet, Indigenous storytelling practices survive and continue to foster resiliency within Indigenous communities. According to Māori scholar Linda Tuhiwai Smith, "'The talk' about the colonial past is embedded in our political discourses, our humour, poetry, music, storytelling, and other common sense ways of passing on both a narrative of history and an attitude about history."[18] Storytelling has been a way for Indigenous Peoples to pass on and keep the culture alive for ages. Before contact with Europeans, stories were passed down from generation to generation to keep Indigenous ceremonies and spirituality strong. As discussed by Jo-Ann Archibald, Indigenous storytelling practices emerge from Indigenous worldviews, using a holistic approach that connects all parts of life—human, animal, plant, and spirit—while weaving together physical, emotional, and spiritual teachings.

Indigenous storytelling practices support both personal health and community balance by including both spiritual and cultural practices, oral traditions, ceremonies, and

---

18   As quoted in Corntassel, 2009, p. 137.

teachings.[19] As such, Indigenous storytelling challenges colonial assimilation by honouring the resilience of teachings within one's culture as they encourage and empower community members to live balanced lives. As Archibald notes,[20] traditional storytelling is often employed as a teaching tool within Indigenous communities.[21] Elders' stories and histories educate communities by passing on Indigenous knowledge and spiritual wisdom in ways that sustain culture, such as respecting the Seven Grandfather Teachings in order to stay in balance spiritually, mentally, physically, and emotionally, as represented on the Medicine Wheel. The Seven Grandfather Teachings are wisdom, love, bravery, honesty, truth, respect, and humility.

My own healing journey and restorying process contributed to the evolution of the Medicine Wheel Tipi model. I've used the Medicine Wheel Tipi (MWT) model for several years as part of my business, as well as making it the focus of my PhD restorying circle project to assist participants in sharing their life stories, starting in the East (childhood years), going to the South (adolescent years), onto the West (adulthood years), and finally to the North (Elderly years). Certain questions or keywords are described within each of the four quadrants of the Medicine Wheel to guide the participants

---

19   Brown & Strega, 2005, p. 252.
20   Archibald, 2008.
21   Archibald, 2008, p. 29.

with their story-sharing. These questions prompt reflection in ways that might lead toward positive self-transformation. The prompts offered in the MWT create conversation and lead participants to think differently about their past histories. The change of thought pattern leads participants to be able to begin to restory their own stories. In addition, the Medicine Wheel Tipi model is designed to encapsulate personal statements relating to their life journeys and prompt them to think not only about the harm they have suffered but also about what one can do to reverse this harm.

Several federal and provincial prison systems have tipis set up on their properties to allow Indigenous Elders to facilitate teachings, which often include discussions of the Medicine Wheel, with incarcerated Indigenous offenders. The MWT was designed to help participants improve their interactions with each other by fostering more open and individualized ways of perceiving situations and problems, provoking new insights through the process of listening to others share their own stories. In my PhD project, the Medicine Wheel Tipi model assisted the participants in remembering their own histories, but in a controlled and sensitive manner.

Participants who've joined sessions through my consulting work have chosen to either burn, throw out, rip up, or never write out their trauma on the side of the Medicine Wheel Tipi intended for this. At one facilitation, a young woman decided not to write on her negative side of the MWT, but I remember her looking at me. I asked her if she wanted to crumple up her MWT and throw it toward me. She said, "Yes." When she threw her MWT, you could see her demeanour and mood change, where she almost immediately looked lighter and happier!

Woolner argues that important lessons can be learned by applying teachings from Elders' stories to one's own life journey. The stories teach respect for self, family members, Elders, communities, neighbours, and all life.[22] Archibald agrees that "some stories powerfully inspire the listeners to make dramatic life changes."[23] Indigenous storytelling offers the opportunity for resiliency and healing within the Indigenous community. This resiliency is an ongoing process where healing transcends trauma, enabling Indigenous Peoples to resist losses of culture and selfhood.[24] Indigenous storytelling practices have always been seen as powerful within Indigenous communities. Storytelling circles may be limited to men, women, or families, but everyone within the group specified is welcome. No one is turned away, ensuring that all have the opportunity not only to listen but to share their own stories and to be part of the stories.

One way storytelling's power is especially evident is in its role within the criminal justice system. While Indigenous storytelling fosters resilience and healing, many Indigenous

---

22 Woolner, 2009, p.3.
23 Archibald, 2008, p. 124.
24 Tousignant & Sioui, 2009, p. 43.

people are disconnected from these traditions until they encounter the justice system—a system that has long been criticized for its colonial and discriminatory treatment of Indigenous Peoples.[25] The respected Ojibwa Elder Art Solomon has famously called the Canadian legal system the "just us" system. Rudin argues that the criminal justice system is built to continue the colonial oppression of Indigenous Peoples,[26] which contributes to the overrepresentation of Indigenous people at all levels of the system. Unfortunately, due to the culturally genocidal effects of systems like residential schools, many Indigenous people are not introduced to their culture until they find themselves involved in the CJS.

It is often during their incarceration that Indigenous offenders begin addressing their spiritual needs and healing by participating in Indigenous programs. However, once they're released, their continued need to stay on the healing path becomes restricted due to the limited Indigenous-specific resources available outside the prison walls, especially in urban areas like Kingston, where there is a small Indigenous population. Within the city of Kingston, there used to be the Katarokwi Native Friendship Centre, but it closed a few years ago. There are only a few remaining Indigenous organizations—including the Métis Nation of Ontario, Kagita Mikam Employment and Training, Tipi Moza housing, and

---

25   Rudin, n.d.; Milloy, 1999.
26   n.d. p.66.

Four Directions, the latter of which primarily serves the Queen's University community but also does some community events—to serve the Indigenous population in Kingston. These Indigenous organizations have limited services to meet the specific needs of Indigenous offenders upon release.

Unfortunately, at the time I was conducting my research, these organizations didn't offer spiritual and cultural ceremonies like sweat lodges or talking circles on a regular basis, which is what Indigenous offenders would benefit the most from. Ironically, these services were more readily available in the prison system. In addition, some Indigenous offenders have found it extremely difficult to seek out the resources they require upon release because they're ashamed or scared to ask for help. For most of their lives, they were told what to do and when and how to do it. They seldom had to look for assistance to help themselves because they were incarcerated, and things were taken care of by other people employed within the criminal justice system, be it in prisons, young offenders' facilities, or group homes.

Upon release, many are forced to articulate their new life journeys alone. Many struggle to create a new story that fits their current release environment, and many end up back on the inside. For some, the same old story keeps creeping back into their lives, entrenching them within the criminal justice system. Many Indigenous people involved with the CJS have experienced some form of intergenerational trauma since childhood. This can be traced back to their individual histories and often to the legacies of the residential school system. The offending circumstances of Indigenous offenders are often related to substance abuse; intergenerational abuse and trauma; residential schools; low levels of education, employment, and income; and substandard housing and health care, among other factors.[27] In addition to dealing with the bureaucracy of the CJS (reporting, curfew, release conditions), Indigenous former offenders may experience intergenerational trauma as overwhelming and destructive to their emotional, psychological, mental, and physical state.

The restorying circle project was designed to provide a safe, supportive, and culturally aware environment in which Indigenous men who have been involved with the CJS can use story to work through what can at times be overwhelming feelings and navigate the tides of trauma to restore balance in all four areas (emotional, physical, mental, and spiritual) reflected in the Medicine Wheel. Too many Indigenous people have become institutionalized, resigning themselves to prison time rather than reclaiming freedom. By encouraging participation in the restorying circles, the goal is to change the attitude and imposed belief that "I belong in prison." Prisoner participation in similar community circles for restorative justice has been demonstrated to reduce the likelihood of reoffending by illustrating to former inmates how their behaviour has impacted victims, families, and communities.[28]

---

27 Spirit Matters, p. 7.
28 Hyatt, 2013, p. 9.

Sharing stories can bring repressed trauma into the light and allow for renewal to begin; we designed restorying to facilitate not only awareness but also rebuilding and affirming identities. The healing journey typically involves identifying areas of change, telling one's story with space for a new Indigenous identity to emerge, analyzing the trauma and links to unhealthy behaviour, and creating a new vision of self where individual healing is part of community healing.[29] The key to this healing journey is the ability to open up a dialogue with oneself and others in a safe and supportive environment in order to discuss the hidden and often damaging incidents that have occurred in one's life and to reflect on these past experiences in a healthy manner. Visiting the past and examining the trauma, an understanding begins to develop of why they do the things they do. A realization surfaces that their current negative behaviour relates, in many cases, to past trauma. Through this realization, a person begins to make healthier choices, leading to positive consequences and healing.

For example, growing up, Peter had the ability to become a good writer; however, due to his harsh upbringing, he didn't have the opportunity to develop this talent. During his years in prison, he began writing and completed a university degree. He said,

---

29   Meseyton, 2005, p. 212.

“ *I had to stifle this for a bit, but my talents shone through throughout my writing periods and when community members asked me to write them something for their college or university. I also wrote stories for my children."*

Here, we see one of the PhD research participants looking inward, nurturing their gifts and strengths, and then using those gifts to strengthen others within his community.

The restorying project showed the importance of creating spaces for supporting Indigenous ex-offenders on their healing journeys. Everyone has a story, and these stories can be changed. No single story sums us up. By participating in circles, Indigenous former offenders gained insights by listening to others' stories and sharing their own. This interweaving of stories within a safe environment with people of similar experiences and backgrounds can encourage participants to view their lives differently, in more balanced and healthy ways. The participants can change harmful ways of thinking and speaking and find renewed ways of storying their lives and identities—focusing on their strengths, gifts, and potential rather than on identities imposed from the outside.

Growing up, these Indigenous participants never had the opportunity to explore their strengths and gifts, as violence and inappropriate role modelling were on display. As children entered school, they often struggled with and were ridiculed for their inability to learn within this education system, topped by the fact that they endured taunts of racism from other non-Indigenous students. These acts of racism were not only in the schoolyard but carried on into the streets of society, where the police began targeting them. These participants have been told that they're hard, tough criminals, that they can't contribute to society, and that they are "less than" because they're Native. They started believing and living this lifestyle, which led to involvement with the criminal justice system.

Over the years of incarceration and introduction to Indigenous cultural and spiritual ceremonies, Indigenous people rediscover their gifts and potential to become who they want to be. These Indigenous programs, culture, and spirituality benefit the Indigenous person by identifying strengths within one's core identity. Alternatively, mainstream Eurocentric culture tends to reflect an opposite system of values, which causes the Indigenous person to struggle and, more importantly, to hide their cultural identity away on the inside. Reclaiming Indigenous identity means recovering traditional values, beliefs, philosophies, ideologies, and approaches and adapting them to what you need for today. This healing begins on the inside and carries through to the outside to one's family and community. As one of the research participants mentioned,

" *It is my life, I look back at it, all those years I was in [prison], I was defined by what other people called me. Who other people told me I was. And I realized there was this one person who wasn't telling me who I was,*

and that was me. And I decided who I was, what I was,
what I was about, what I was going to think, what I
was going to do, how I was going to do it, it was my
decision from now on."

When participants share experiences that were previously held back, they gain clarity to reinterpret incidents in ways that can change their lives.[30] Restorying also creates space for challenging the narratives of Canadian history and rewriting historical narratives to acknowledge past injustices and foster reconciliation.[31] Restorying means creating spaces where Indigenous people can take back their voices and begin to piece together identities that have been fragmented by colonial oppression—fragmentation that has been exacerbated by incarceration. In doing so, they transform stories of victimhood into stories of resiliency to heal from intergenerational trauma.

Through my dissertation, I wanted to implement a process that supports Indigenous people in generating hope and healing through storytelling. Although limited by funding and time, my PhD project supported participants while adding knowledge about resilience, restorying, and potential pathways for policy change and community action. This restorying circle project was an innovative initiative toward

---

30 Rosenthal, 2003, p. 923.
31 Woolner, 2009, p. 39.

healing to calm the waves of trauma suffered by Indigenous communities and their members. When a person is asked to remember, they're also being asked to create.

The act of remembering is fundamentally creative within a story-sharing environment because the person remembering chooses what from their history to share and how to share it; participants ultimately have control over the stories they tell about themselves and their histories. They are not just victims of their histories, but rather, they are empowered to a certain degree to understand those histories in ways that work for them. They're creative agents and not just passive victims. As participant Laine describes,

> " *My childhood as I try to reflect on it, sometimes I have a hard time remembering the good things, and a lot of the bad things stand out more, but I question it more and more each day, and a lot of times I try to focus on the good things in my life that I'm doing today.*"

Remembering and revitalizing our consciousness in a healthy manner (within a restorying circle amid the support of others) permits individuals to endorse their own agency to reframe their histories in a positive context. This creation and restorying has an important healing element. History is an interpretive event as much as memory is a story we construct. As Peter says,

❝ *We learn from stories, from the Elders, ourselves, from our relations, our kids. And it's true, we heal from them. This has been a safe place for telling stories, which is good. Our lodges are the same thing. And I've realized that with a core group of people, a core group of brothers in there, you can say anything. And you know you're going to be safe. And they're going to support you. Even in prison, where they say you can't have any friends. Or you can't trust who's inside with you."*

P. R. Krech agrees that "storytelling, talking circles...and community based spiritual ceremony have begun to find inroads into the process of 're-storying' one's life, thereby bringing about a reframed sense of 'self'."[32] I agree that the safety and support of the restorying circles were critical to helping the participants open up about their pasts and start the restorying process. The spiritual and cultural parts of the circles are important. But the participants' knowledge and understanding are just as crucial in helping them think about their past and move toward a "reframed sense of 'self.'" The most important part of their success was the sense of community and support developed among the men in our restorying circles.

---

32   Krech, 2002, p. 90.

My goal for my PhD research was to highlight how the stories shared by the participants illustrate many of the common aspects of intergenerational trauma: early experiences with abuse, dysfunctional families or foster care, substance abuse and addiction, isolation, lack of positive role models and schooling, and poverty. As expected, many of their experiences involved harsh, isolating, and traumatic events, which led to negative peer influences and negative choices such as substance abuse, and eventually incarceration. Although these narratives seem inevitable and predictable, they were not the only stories shared. Each story was unique and interwoven with glimpses of hope and positive memories, teaching us that restorying isn't a simple process of replacing negative perspectives with a positive outlook but that stories, like life itself, are complex and ever-changing.

Although most of the participant stories I share involve the criminal justice system, the method is applicable in many settings. The majority of the groups that we offer this to are not just people involved in the criminal justice system, but those trying to help people either stay out of the criminal justice system, not go back to the criminal justice system, or choose a different path. One participant said, "[From] something so bad, comes something so good. I was stuck for a really long time and then became unstuck." My company, Life-Circle Consulting, has worked with the City of Kingston's Housing and Social Services Department and the HomeBridge Youth Society in Halifax, Nova Scotia, where they help out Indigenous and non-Indigenous youth in a group home setting. We have worked with the entire mental health and addiction department of Nishnawbe Aski Nation (NAN). NAN represents forty-nine First Nations with a total population (on- and off-reserve) of approximately 45,000 people grouped by Tribal Council.

We've offered training to the Thunder Woman Healing Lodge in Toronto, comprised of over thirty workers. Rainbow Lodge, one of Ontario's few Indigenous treatment facilities offering addiction and mental health services, has adopted our "restorying your story" into their recovery program. We have also worked with the Listuguj First Nation education department in northern New Brunswick. We offered this training to the Mi'kmaw Legal Support Network (MLSN), which was initiated by the Nova Scotia Chiefs to develop and maintain a sustainable justice support system. Finally, we have also offered our services to individuals who are struggling with their own stories.

In our workshops, participants have shared stories of pain and trauma and allowed the secrets of shame, abuse, and suffering to be revealed. They have supported each other in recognizing strength, resilience, and opportunities for growth and healing. In addition, the Elders and facilitators have listened and can share wisdom, prayers, and hope.

It's important to look back and understand where we've come from before going forward. Let me share with you more of my own story. You will see that I grew up in poverty and violence, negatively impacted by the effects of residential schools and involved with the child welfare system, like so many Indigenous people impacted by colonialism. These collective experiences have led us to similar paths. However, unlike so many others, I had the opportunity, support, and privilege to get out of the cycle of incarceration. I restoried my life. Unfortunately, so many Indigenous people don't get this same chance due to their own circumstances. I'll show how I got out of this cycle and restoried my life, an action that I hope inspires others to do the same.

The Early
Chapters

From the ages of four to eight, I was placed in and out of foster homes.

At the age of eight, I moved to Prince Edward Island, leaving my mother behind in Toronto. My father gave us up for adoption, and then I moved to Germany with my adoptive family.

I read my child welfare documents due to the fact of being part of the Sixties Scoop claim, which showed how my mother could not be located, so the judge just took away her consent and gave me and my siblings up for adoption. I remember thinking for many years about how my mother never loved me and that I was unlovable. In my early twenties, I discovered my mother had five other kids in another family up in Northern Ontario. All those times she took off, and all these years, I was thinking one thing when, in actuality, she was just trying to be a good mother to all of us within her own addiction struggles and abusive past.

I experienced isolation due to being disconnected from family and culture when I moved to Germany and lived with an abusive adoptive family. Upon reflection of my story, two things stick out in my mind. The first is that I would go to the library a lot. Most of you would think this is a good thing, but in reality, I went there because I was embarrassed and hid as I had no lunches to eat. Even though I went to the library to hide, I actually learned to appreciate reading books.

The second thing that sticks out in my memory from that time is I buried myself in the game of Ping-Pong. I would play it every single chance I could as another form of escape. Through my education process and research, I learned that playing Ping-Pong was a form of self-imposed eye movement therapy to deal with traumatic experiences.

I know firsthand that residential schools had a direct impact on what type of mom I had and the parenting I received. Most people who attended residential schools never witnessed or experienced positive parenting, affection, or kindness from an adult. I believe the emotional, physical, spiritual, and sexual abuse that my mother endured in those schools shaped how she treated and interacted with us, her children. She simply had no idea how to be a good mom. I do know one thing that she was good at—my mother would drink a lot to forget her demons and would then disappear. The residential school abuse that my mother experienced was passed onto me and my siblings through another form of colonization termed "intergenerational trauma," which I personally had to overcome through my own struggles.

I was disconnected from my family, my community, and even my own identity after being placed in foster homes and eventually adopted. Colonization directly impacted my mother, then me, and, to some extent, even my children. It's like colonization was a machine gun, firing bullets to annihilate First Nations people. These bullets hit countless children, who grew up and passed on these wounds to the next several generations. These stories of pain caused by the bullets of colonization (residential schools), have been heard over the last hundred years, but now we are starting to tell stories of resiliency, survival, and thriving again.

Suffering harsh treatment growing up, supported by negative stories of isolation, poverty, drug abuse, and violence, the Indigenous men participating in my PhD study unsurprisingly became embroiled in the criminal justice system. These negative experiences impacted the stories these men initially shared in our circles, often negatively describing themselves as wounded like the eagle and feeling like they don't belong. They learned life lessons from their peers within the criminal justice system. These stories often took them further from a core of cultural identity, family, and personhood. They learned to behave in different ways, to present themselves in other ways, to cope in various ways, and to align themselves with expectations about carceral masculinities, indigeneity, and power. Keeping their eyes to the ground like a chicken pecking seeds, the Indigenous participants in this study described being conditioned to perform identities that they never fully claimed —identities at odds with stories they would ultimately tell about their gifts, aspirations, and cultural rootedness. Such dissonance can be experienced as alienation from oneself and one's family. One participant explained how, after his release from prison, "Every time [he] saw a family member, [he]'d take off in the opposite direction because [he] didn't want to be around [his] people, I guess because of their lack of care or concern." Yet each participant expressed a desire to reconnect with Indigenous culture and community, a common aspiration of Indigenous Peoples grappling with ongoing settler colonialism, as argued by Susan Dion in *Braiding Histories*.[33]

---

33 Dion, 2009, p. 22.

Colonialism and its Impacts

My mother attended Horton Hall residential school in Moose Factory and was given a number to replace her name. She suffered sexual and physical abuse at the school. Years later, alcohol was her only known form of "medication," which she abused. She eventually died young as a result. She did not know how to parent us as she never witnessed any form of healthy parenting staying at the school. My brothers and sisters were raised in a very abusive environment.

I have so many negative associations with the word *colonization*. For me, colonization started when the *Indian Act* was created to control First Nations peoples in Canada. Its ultimate goal wasn't to turn First Nations people into Europeans—it was to annihilate us. To me, colonization is a term that basically means erasure—getting rid of a group of people whom the colonizers felt weren't human or equal to them; therefore, they were expendable.

When you examine the *Indian Act*, it is about control and provides the means for the government to dictate what a First Nations person can or cannot do in this country. Through colonization, the implementation of the treaties would take away the majority of the lands from the stewardship of First

Nations people. Many of the treaties were deceitful because what was written in the treaties was not necessarily what First Nations signatories had verbally agreed to.

One of the most destructive tools of colonization was the creation of residential schools. Their primary purpose was not to educate or improve children's lives, but to destroy their First Nations identity, culture, and language. These institutions functioned like factories, changing identity. They took kids who lived off the land, practiced their culture, took part in ceremony, spoke their own languages, ate traditional foods, and dressed in their own way—and tried to destroy them. The colonizers took these children and attempted to kill them, destroy them, erase them, or turn them into Europeans.

Instead of receiving affection or education, First Nations children were subjected to abuse and labour. They were physically, sexually, emotionally, mentally, and spiritually punished just because they were different. Upon arrival at the schools, the young children had their clothes ripped off their backs, their hair was cut short, and they were transformed into looking like the colonizer. These schools were purposely built in places that were far enough away from First Nations communities so that students' families were unable to visit and check in on them to make sure that they were okay. When the children did return home for the holidays or the summer breaks, many struggled to fit back into their First Nations communities. Many had forgotten how to speak their own language, leaving them unable to communicate with their families. There was a sense over time that they no longer felt like they belonged—neither in their First Nations families and communities nor in the colonizer's world.

Therefore, they felt that they could no longer fit into life in general. Many students suffered all forms of abuse—they never experienced healthy affection from the teachers, priests, or nuns. They were never given proper role modelling for how to treat each other with respect, love, and kindness. After their time at the schools and into adulthood, they passed on this terrible treatment to other people. As parents, they mistreated their children because they had only experienced negativity themselves. This was all part of the process of colonization: to attack the identity, disconnect from family, and abuse the soul, leading to poverty, unemployment, violence, drug addiction, and lack of privilege or opportunity for First Nations people.

Another mode of colonization's attack is the child welfare system, which worked in parallel to the residential school system in the late 1960s to early 1970s, when the residential schools were no longer as effective at carrying out the duties of colonization. The child welfare system had the ability to remove First Nations children and place them in homes far away from the First Nations communities. This practice continued until at least the late 1990s. This period of time is referenced as the 60's Scoop because of how they would scoop (take) Indigenous children from their families. The power of colonization in this country is strong. I keep thinking about how the government was allowed to remove children from the parents' homes, and if the parents tried to interfere, they could go to prison. I can't comprehend why other countries in this world could allow such a thing, but this was what happened in Canada.

The media has also shaped Canadians' views of Indigenous Peoples by presenting them as inferior and reinforcing stereotypes such as that of "the drunken Indian" incapable of holding a job or creating a healthy family and community.

Colonization has had a catastrophic effect on Indigenous Peoples. When you look at many of the First Nations communities in this country, you can see how colonization has left its path of destruction in the community, the family, and the individual. The history and disastrous effects of colonization over time have left many Indigenous people in this country feeling a sense of imbalance and a lack of physical, mental, emotional, and spiritual well-being.

Over the next seven generations, colonization and its goal of destroying Indigenous cultures and peoples lost the battle. It did not achieve its goal, as Indigenous Peoples' cultures, languages, ways of life, and ways of knowing are winning out over colonization.

Yet, colonialism and its tools—residential schools, child welfare, and intergenerational trauma—have impacted the self, family, and community for many Indigenous people. These experiences impact one's narrative, which gets played over and over every day. The following list of topics is part of an exercise we carry out in the restorying circles, guiding people to realize how the negative impact of these colonial systems has an impact on their own story. For each heading, we ask what sorts of concepts it involves, and a list is generated, much like the list below. More importantly, when you write down the words, you can get an idea of what needs to happen to restory these negative words. For example, under "Residential Schools," we have "No love." It follows that feeling and sharing love is the way to restory this experience. Under "Intergenerational Trauma," we see "Loss of language." Therefore, learning our language is one way to restory our story.

I included my story above to help you better understand how this would fall under the "Residential Schools" section, under "Family system destroyed."

Residential Schools

1. No love
2. No parenting
3. Lack of identity
4. Violence
5. Substance abuse
6. Physical or sexual abuse
7. Family system destroyed
8. Oppression
9. No trust
10. Addiction
11. Division
12. Lack of understanding and compassion

Child Welfare

1. Still want to be with their real parents
2. Loss of identity and culture
3. Mistreated (abused, no love)
4. No sense of belonging
5. Creates dependency
6. Unhealthy
7. Missed cultural education

Intergenerational Trauma

1. Parents taken away—Missed out on affection, love, and nurturing
2. Sexual abuse
3. Lack of culture
4. Loss of identity
5. Loss of language
6. Trauma carried forward
7. Experience trauma
8. Lateral violence institutionalized
9. Problems in mental, physical, spiritual, and emotional areas
10. Denial of status—disbelief

Loneliness and Isolation

For restorying participants, isolating themselves was a choice or escape made out of necessity and self-preservation against the violence of their family members, who are supposed to love them and provide a sense of belonging. However, through self-isolation, the person no longer has others to provide support, nurture them, and offer guidance on life directions. What eventually happens is that this isolation seeps into this person's identity and begins to fester by speaking negative thoughts like "I'm not worthy of friends," "I don't deserve a family," and "I don't need support and love." Feelings like these often lead to negative behaviour such as drug/alcohol abuse, committing crime, and possibly suicide.

Ironically, the main purpose of the shield of isolation was initially to protect the child from violence often informed by substance abuse; however, these very same social factors later become manifest in the person's adolescent and adult lives as they commit acts of violence toward others and themselves, mostly under the influence of substances. Isolation, loneliness, and despair are all words that describe the participants' lives growing up as young people; these same words also describe the feelings of many who attempt suicide.

So many young people—especially Indigenous youth—feel alone, that nobody loves them, and that life isn't fair, leading to thoughts of suicide. These young people have often been forced into isolation by society and family dysfunction, and they use isolation as a shield for their protection; however, as time goes on, this shield increases their sense of abandonment, cutting them off from their families and communities. Cut off from a circle of love and support. Many are left with only alcohol and drugs to numb their pain.

Feelings of isolation and loneliness led these participants toward criminal behaviours due to boredom, lack of structure, and hanging out with the wrong crowd, eventually leading to incarceration. The experiences of loneliness and isolation were further entrenched by segregation within the prison system. Loneliness and isolation were learned behaviours and normal for the participants, so once they became imprisoned, they didn't have a feeling of shock or discomfort—perhaps the opposite occurred.

One of the most striking commonalities among the participants' stories in my PhD project of their early years was the *frequency* of experiences of loneliness and isolation. At a young age, loneliness began, and it continued throughout most of the participants' teenage years.

"My growing up was loneliness," said one participant. "That's the one thing I remember was being alone." At school, several struggled to focus on their learning, were bullied by others, and were distracted because of home life problems. In most cases, family members neglected these participants instead of getting them involved in social groups and activities. Anger often surfaced without consistent guidance from their parents or guardians, and as children, the participants often acted out their emotions in ways that got them in trouble with the school or the law.

Within the restorying circles, the participants described multiple layers of isolation that became naturalized over time. One layer emerged for multiple participants when they had to seek safety from violent and intoxicated family members or acquaintances as children. A second layer occurred as participants became acclimatized to their youthful solitude. One participant claimed, "My mom said it years ago to me. She said, 'It's how you were. You were always alone.'" A third layer involved feelings of shame and guilt about circumstances, which led participants to withdraw from others and thereby avoid people asking questions. A fourth layer often involved a tactical escape from difficult experiences by seeking refuge in drugs and alcohol, which further separated participants from others. A fifth layer involved being labelled as "criminal" and distanced from family and others. "I stole a lot of gas," said one participant. "Stealing the gas, or break into the Hudson Bay or Co-op, to get some more money for gambling, for drugs, gas, booze. The cops came to me later because they knew me." The final layer segregating the participants from family, community, and society involved the isolation of incarceration.

Peter said, "My adolescence, I start moving away from people, [from] having friends." This type of isolation can stunt social skill development. Also, some participants described feeling unloved by their family members, which led to feelings of loneliness. Some participants had to escape from their homes just to avoid being hurt by their family members. The violence in the home made the participants feel embarrassed and ashamed, which contributed to their sense of isolation. Another participant shared, "I felt the best when I was alone and in the bush." The participants' loneliness was exacerbated in some cases by the thought that they were the only person suffering from the abuse and nobody was there to help.

Few of my PhD research participants grew up experiencing trusting relationships with love, kindness, understanding, and respect. People have a better chance to develop trust by having their personal needs met growing up. The ability to trust and have trust reciprocated was not developed through experience within most of the participants' lives. We tend to trust someone whose actions correspond with their words. The participants didn't trust others because, in their experience, people's actions seldom aligned with their words. In the words of one participant,

66 *I didn't know anything about trust because that was taken away from me...when I was a younger individual."*

Research has suggested that trust has been diminished at different levels in First Nations communities.[34] Thibodeau

34 Thibodeau & Peigan, 2007, p. 50.

and Peigan say that lower levels of trust come from the historical trauma and oppression First Nations people faced.[35] As suggested by the participants, there was a lack of trust at a personal level. Aphrodite Matsakis explains how trauma affects self-trust.

> " *Trauma survivors not only lost trust in some of the basic premises that kept people functioning such as the assumptions of personal invulnerability and that the world is just and fair but they can also lose trust in people, including themselves.*"[36]

Many participants in my PhD study said they were unable to turn to their family members for support. This was due to fear of maltreatment and victimization within the family. As a result of decades of Canadian policies rooted in assimilation and genocide, many Indigenous people have been mistreated and dishonoured within their families. This led to diminished levels of trust within that domain.[37]

Trust was broken many times in the participants' lives, which impacted their perceptions of relationships with others. Some participants were told not to trust anyone. Ryan, for instance, told us, "I remember my dad taught me, 'You can't

---

35   Thibodeau & Pegan, 2007.
36   Matsakis, 1998, p.57.
37   Thibodeau & Peigan, 2007, p. 51.

trust them. They're not your friends.'" Some participants did not trust authority figures. David recalled, "The police were bad, anybody with authority was bad, the teachers were the authorities, and from what I had seen, they were all bad." Peter never spoke to correctional staff for five years while incarcerated due to his lack of trust in authorities.

Growing up, the messages and stories engrained in the participants' minds were not to trust anyone but to take care of things themselves. One participant noted,

> *" I was very leery of anybody who wanted to be my friend. I was very untrusting of people. I realize that I had this need that I wanted friends, but I also realized that those people who said they were my friends were never my friends."*

As a result of this distrust, some Indigenous people have experienced a limited ability to be open, share, and contribute to themselves and family.[38]

Feelings of disconnection were exacerbated by experiences with drugs and alcohol and unhealthy relationships on the streets. As one participant said, "No one cared for me, and I didn't care what happened to me either." To survive, these men did not allow other possible role models, such as teachers, to get close or be an influence.

---

38 Thibodeau & Peigan, 2007, p. 57

Isolation, Substance Abuse, and Incarceration

For many years, I never spoke about all the trauma that I suffered. I carried this trauma silently, never sharing my negative narrative with anyone. Looking back, I guess it would have been helpful to speak with someone who could have supported me. At the time, I felt all alone, as if nobody cared for or loved me. But there was always something in me that made me believe that there was hope—that my life could get better.

Unfortunately, I never dealt with all the unhealthy stuff that was going on in my life in an effective way. So, when I started drinking, it became my gateway to the criminal justice system. At first, I didn't realize it, but eventually, I started to unleash the trauma. When I drank, I would end up in fights all the time. A few times, I would drink and drive, but more often, I just got kicked out of bars for fighting. In a way, alcohol gave me the permission to unleash the trauma that I experienced as a kid onto others. If I had the opportunity to really sit down and get help from a person who cared, I believe my life would have been a lot different.

Like my own experience, isolation, substance abuse, and incarceration contributed to each of the participants' inability to address his past issues, making it difficult for him to share his stories in a positive manner. The stories of the men involved in our circles tended to demonstrate causal relationships among isolation, substance abuse, and eventual incarceration. Each of the participants' lives was impacted negatively by substance abuse. As Laine expressed,

> *I always remember my family, father, mother, and uncles were always drinking. They were all partying, and so did we. I started smoking more and more and more, and drinking more and more."*

The participants thought nothing was wrong with abusing substances as they witnessed their parents and other family members engage in these behaviours.

Participants described how experiences of loneliness came to be internalized as unworthiness and despair, which affected their life stories as they grew older. Many participants shared negative experiences of not fitting in at school. Ryan described how "every day at school was a constant struggle. And school I didn't like because there were bad teachers. I wasn't doing anything. School was boring." They spoke about instances of violence and attacks by other students: "I got my ass handed to me a number of times on the school yard."

One participant described being given an ultimatum by the principal to stay in class or to leave school for good. He told of lighting up a cigarette in front of the principal and walking out the doors of the school—he quit. However, for others within the study, the school was a safe place to escape from a volatile home life. Laine articulated, "I used to love going to school because it was getting me out of the house, away from my father. I was there just to kill time to get away from my mother's place because she was drinking more because of her addiction."

In every case, the participants in my PhD research study dropped out of school before grade 10, largely due to their negative experiences at school and at home. Ryan said, "I quit high school. I just turned 16. I was in grade 9. I walked away from it pretty quick." The school experience surrounding bullying, violence, failing in class, and not fitting in with their fellow students influenced the lives of the participants negatively as they grew up.

Participants reported often having abused illegal substances to deal with past trauma, loneliness, and isolation. Abusing substances meant becoming involved with criminal activity for these men, eventually leading to incarceration. Dependence upon illegal substances was a contributing factor leading to break and enters, thefts, and other offences. David explained, "I was starting to get in a lot of trouble with the law for sniffing and starting smoking, hash, a lot of break and enters." The participants' crimes were often forms of theft to gain money for alcohol or drugs. Ryan revealed,

" *I'm the one who started breaking into houses, stealing to make the money so that we could drink. And once, when I had no money, I decided to rob people on the street. This was my first encounter with the law. I got pinched doing a robbery with violence one evening."*

Most of the participants started abusing drugs and alcohol early in life. All participants committed their crimes to feed their substance abuse habits. For some, sniffing gasoline also became a problem. This behaviour led them to young offenders' facilities or group homes. Laine recalls, "I was too young, sniffing lots of gas and glue. I started with gas, then there was anything they could get their hands on." Similar experiences are identified by Latimer and Foss, who mention that "in the year 2000 the rate of incarceration for Aboriginal youth was 64.5 per 10,000 population, as compared to 8.2 per 10,000 population for non-Aboriginal youth, and 8 out of 10 incarcerated Aboriginal youth had a substance abuse problem."[39]

These participants in the restorying circles reported continuing to abuse substances in prison, as drugs were as prevalent on the inside as the outside. Peter describes that "it was not uncommon to watch some guys drop 27 to 30 hits of acid at a time when the drug came into the institution. Valium use was not uncommon, where 75 to 100 ten milligram pills were eaten every day." Peter told of having overdosed in prison seven times due, as he explained, to his desire to get higher each time he took the drugs. He was dubbed

---

[39] Latimer & Foss, 2004, p.3.

a "functional addict" by prison authorities. According to an inmate survey, 34% of offenders admitted to injection drug use prior to incarceration and 11% indicated they have injected since they have been in custody; in addition, 25% of inmates reported that they are under pressure to smuggle drugs into the institution.[40]

My participants rarely shared their feelings while incarcerated. Prison is not the place for reflection and opening up about such emotions. It's not a place to seek support, share feelings, or seek acceptance from others. If a person decided to open up about his feelings regarding isolation, he would likely be picked on and isolated from the inmate population. Prisoners often develop and wear masks of hypermasculinity. This performance helps to prevent other prisoners from sensing their vulnerability. Offenders take on false senses of self as a way of protection, as they don't want to be harmed for portraying their genuine identities. Instead, inmates must deal with false selves and negative expectations that can lead to self-destructive thoughts and behaviours. Inmates are then encouraged to avoid others, which makes loneliness worse.[41]

Such feelings of loneliness and isolation continued for a majority of the PhD research participants in this study upon their release from prison. Upon release, most did not have the

---

40 McVie, n.d., para 2.
41 Psychalive, 2016, para 2.

support of family and friends because of their past offences. Shame and guilt were experienced by the offenders, which prevented them from wanting to go out into the community and build new relationships. Also, some of the relationships developed inside the prison no longer exist because some offenders are prohibited from hanging around others with criminal records. A special condition can be imposed by the Parole Board of Canada, which requires the former offender not to associate with anyone they know or has reason to believe is involved in criminal activity.[42] The absence of a strong network of support within the community upon release created conditions in which recidivism was highly probable for many of the participants. Laine reflected,

" *My adult years, and that's where I got caught up in the system more. Then I started getting stuck in the federal system. It's like, where'd my twenties go, where'd my thirties go? I lost it all. I started to get lost in the system. It's like a haze to me.*"

These men experienced incarceration for an extensive period of their lives. Peter served over 30 years inside the prison system at various federal institutions across the country and at different security levels: "I have approximately eight years maximum time, twenty years medium time,

---

42 Kings County Advertiser, Conditions Imposed section, para 6.

and four years minimum time." In a similar manner to how they described becoming comfortable with being alone as children and youth, most participants described becoming comfortable with incarceration and institutionalization. Laine said, "It's just the way I lived my life at that time I guess, in and out of prison, jails." This experience was connected to his realization: "I grew up with the understanding of loneliness."

The participants often escaped the harshness of their realities on the outside by turning to substance abuse. Laine explained:

> *I didn't even know at that time that the choices I was making were the beginning of my incarcerations. You know the downward spiral. All the hurt, shame, guilt, the things that I've seen I didn't want to believe was actually happening. It hurt to realize that it was real. What was I doing? I was just adding more fuel to the fire and running away from my own problems. And getting involved with drugs and alcohol and eventually growing up in the system as a young offender [who] turned into an adult."*

Sharing their stories, many of the PhD research participants demonstrated marked self-reflexivity about the relationship between their experiences of trauma, chosen methods of escapism like drugs and alcohol, and further isolation through incarceration. Laine poignantly reflected on the ways in which chosen methods for coping with the "hurt, shame [and] guilt" of personal experiences too troubling to "believe" they were "actually happening" actually ended up exacerbating the difficulties—"adding more fuel to the fire." The downward spiral guided this man toward institutionalization and incarceration. The participants also mastered over time the skill of incarceration. Laine described,

> *I think about it now, I was actually comfortable inside these open custodies and secure custody places as a young offender."*

The toxic prison environment no longer had an effect on him, as it seemed much better than living on the streets. Sure, he was incarcerated, isolated, and still embroiled in substance abuse, but he no longer had to worry about having enough to eat, about finding work, about ensuring he had a place to sleep. As Peter put it, "You get three meals a day and everything else you want." However, over time, the participants described how prison weighed on them, leading them eventually to desire something different, something better. Peter explained,

> *I found out I had a chance to get out of prison. Prior to this, I just figured I would live my whole life there, and I would eventually die. This changed for me and I really began working on myself."*

Carceral Trauma and the Heightening of Isolation

The men shared how their experiences of trauma, caused by personal isolation and other negative social factors, led them to make negative choices such as dropping out of school, breaking the law, and using drugs. Which then heightened the chances of future incarceration. These experiences must be viewed in the larger picture of how Indigenous Peoples in Canada face marginalization. Ongoing settler colonialism increases their risk of violence and abuse. According to Laforme, "The long-term consequences of trauma among Indigenous Peoples include intergenerational ineffective parenting; poverty; unemployment; substance abuse; low levels of education; and the widespread acceptance that violence is the norm."[43] These conditions show why Indigenous people are overrepresented in the prison system. They also shape the lives of the men in this study.

Poverty, violence, and lack of employment created and reinforced isolating behaviour among our PhD research

---

43   Laforme, 2005, p.17.

participants. Many of the men spoke about their experiences of loneliness and isolation in their home lives and experiences of schooling. These become further complicated when we take into account how the criminal justice system disciplines them. An immediate consequence of incarceration is the loss of personal control over daily decisions.[44] As Indigenous former inmate Yvonne Johnson gravely adds:

> " *The people who have control of your stories, control of your voice, also have control of your destiny, your culture.*"[45]

The strict limits on personal choice also impacted what little sense of control the men felt over their own lives and futures. They were told what to do and how to do it, either by the guards or by other prisoners who were higher in the prisoner hierarchy. As Peter shared, "My crime placed me at the top next to the cop killers, bank robbers."

In these ways, the participants in this study described how the isolation they experienced as youth was intensified by their experiences of incarceration, in which they were discouraged from being vulnerable and self-expressive, were controlled via the power structure of carceral discipline, and were disconnected physically and emotionally from family

---

44 Haney, 2001, p. 7.
45 Rymhs, 2008, p. 55.

members and loved ones. The prison is often perceived as an unwelcoming environment, which prevents many family members and others from choosing to visit. Many offenders' only connection with loved ones is over a limited phone call with other prisoners nearby listening in.

This structural discouragement of family connection inside the prison system functions to further isolate offenders, as described by Laine:

66 *My mother came to visit me a couple of times, but there were times when I reached out to her, and no one was there. That's when I started to feel like I was abandoned. I just became lost pretty much.*"

Role Models

My internal narrative started to change at the age of nineteen, when I started speaking up for myself, no longer staying quiet, and I decided not to live in fear. I had hit my rock bottom when it came to allowing others to hurt me. And my internal narrative also had enough. I wanted to have a better life and treatment by others. Earlier, I mentioned I called this internal narrative "Little Mike," the parentified child who was always afraid to rock the boat and upset others. Changing this internal narrative is an ongoing process that continues to this day, but I must add that it does not take as long to change the internal narrative from negative to positive now as it did before.

I think one of my big influences for this change had to be my friend's father, who was good to me. When I first met him, I was in grade 9 and I would hang around his home and have him display positive role modelling toward me. I felt like he treated me like his own son, which I deeply appreciate now more than I did before. Unfortunately, when I graduated from high school, I left Oromocto and I no longer had a relationship with him. However, the healthy imprinting he left on me played a significant role in my wanting to do better. His positive influence on me helped to steer me in a positive and healthy direction years later after I quit drinking. Without his positive role modelling, I would still be in a destructive environment.

I also know that playing sports and my teammates really helped me. Sports was my safe place and my medicine, even though I did not realize it at the time. I think sports and playing Ping-Pong gave me the therapy I required to get through so many tough times. Sports helped me do the restorying of my negative story a lot of the time.

Positive role modelling is vital during childhood. It helps children learn what appropriate behaviour looks like. Also, positive role models aid in forming aspirational projections for their future selves. Yet, such role modelling was missing in the lives of most PhD research participants. On the contrary, negative role modelling impacted the participants' childhood and teenage years, encouraging poor decisions and behaviours. In some cases, this then led to incarceration and negatively affected individuals' futures. There were limited learning opportunities and experiences through role modelling to encourage success for many participants. The absence of positive role models experienced by the participants in this study aligns with Hyatt's research findings, which suggest that Indigenous inmates tend to have fewer positive role models than non-Indigenous people.[46] Some participants recalled having minimal positive interactions

---

46   Hyatt Research, 2013, p.43.

with their fathers during their early years. "I couldn't ask my dad anything because right away I should know this stuff," one participant shared, "and well, when you're a kid, you don't know anything."

Children, growing up, imitate the behaviour they witness. Many of the participants described imitating negative behaviours observed in terms of violence and substance abuse. As one participant mentioned, "My parents and relatives were all partying, so we joined them and partied as well." Another participant described witnessing his dad beat up his mother. Laine said poignantly,

> " *I used to look up to him until I saw him doing that first violent stuff to my mother. I loved this man, I looked up to him as a role model, but it started to change. It's like colouring a picture, going from white to grey to black."*

The participant's father, his role model and hero, becomes the enemy, turning from white to black. The use of colours eloquently illustrates the evolving relationship between the participant and his father: The colour black portrays the harmful role modelling instilled into this participant, which would not only destroy trust and love but also increase isolation and feelings of hopelessness. A participant shared in the circle, "I felt powerless when I witnessed violence against my mom and siblings but could do nothing to change the situation." This allowed feelings of anger to grow and solidified the role of the victim. Unfortunately, as this participant acknowledged, the cycle continued as he was involved in domestic violence in later life.

As young teenagers, most of the participants started hanging around criminal associates who might be considered bad role models. Two participants shared how they learned their life lessons while incarcerated. Ryan recalls,

> *[I] met a guy named [Mike] at the jail, who sat me down. He said, 'This is the way you do things, kid.' And I followed that, all these years. I met [him] on the street years later, we drank together, partied together, and we laughed together."*

Laine shared that,

> *People that I met inside that got released ahead of me. I met up with them, and the streets were my newfound friend. They were drug dealers."*

However, as the stories of these participants show, it's never too late to seek out positive role models in their lives. Like Elders, who, in some cases, were introduced to these participants while incarcerated. Peter told the group, "This is when I met Art Solomon. And he planted a seed as far as my spirituality was concerned. Elders came into the brotherhood on a regular occasion, and I found myself talking to them." Elders play a role in the healing process by providing cultural histories and traditional teachings. This is frequently reported to be the reason that many Indigenous inmates reconnect to their cultural identities.[47]

Despite having few positive role models in their lives as younger men, these participants described wanting to give back to the youth and become better role models themselves. The expressed goal was to prevent these youth from going to prison. As Peter expressed,

> *I can share my story with them and hope they can learn something. I can empathize with them and how they feel—the loneliness, despair, and the reasons for using drugs or alcohol. I will not judge them; I can listen and will listen. I may not have solutions much of the time, but we share common problems."*

The protocols established in these restorying circles can be used as a template, allowing participants to revisit past life experiences with an intent to heal, restore, and redirect in a healthy direction. Furthermore, providing a safe, culturally appropriate space to meet may well be integral to fostering a supportive and mutually accountable community for this marginalized group. There are many Indigenous organizations throughout urban centres in Canada that offer cultural programs, Elder services, and welcoming spaces that could adopt this restorying circle project into their regular

---

47   Wilson, 2002; Nielsen, 2003.

activities, with the particular goal of serving the healing needs of Indigenous people whose lives have been embroiled in the CJS. Some of the ones I've worked with, and mentioned throughout this book, include the Thunder Woman Healing Lodge in Toronto and the Mi'kmaw Legal Support Network.

Many of the participants suffered from colonialism, common amongst Indigenous people within the CJS. Rather than feeling blame, shame, guilt, or isolation, participants are encouraged to realize that their experiences are all too common. Through sharing and listening to personal stories, the participants begin to develop hope and see their survival and resilience as strength. They come to recognize that they're not defined by what they have been told or by their prison labels, but by the gifts they have to offer, as illustrated by the eagle story.

However, I was surprised by how seldom the participants contextualize their experiences within a colonial framework or view their incarceration within a broader history of Indigenous dispossession, assimilation, and containment in Canada.

The written history of Canada shares how explorers from Europe (mainly French and English) "discovered" this country to claim its resources for their home countries. They found Indigenous Peoples already here, but appropriated the land and resources through violence, disease, government policies (including the *Indian Act*), laws, and treaties. These histories speak of how the country was colonized, "civilized," and settled, but ignore the stories of the people who were already living on the land, how the explorers and settlers treated them, and how they were continually dispossessed in ways that included the repeatedly compromised treaties.

This colonial framework has been violently reinforced through practices like residential schooling, the removal of Indigenous Peoples to reserves, and the overrepresentation of Indigenous people in the criminal justice system. The colonial framework naturalizes these acts of dispossession and genocide by perpetuating the belief that Indigenous Peoples are inferior and ignorant, and therefore criminal and irredeemable. A component of intergenerational trauma is the internalization of these beliefs by Indigenous People themselves, as well as the frequent personal and community exposure to prejudice and discrimination.

There were no direct questions regarding this colonial framework and how it related to the participants' lives within the restorying circles. However, upon listening to the participants' stories, there's a direct correlation between their past negative treatment by their family members and the historical discriminatory and assimilation policies of the colonial framework. You can see how and why these participants, and other Indigenous people, are perfect candidates for the criminal justice system: poverty, limited education, unavailable employment, high rates of substance abuse, the epidemic of Indigenous suicide, and high rates of crime are all connected to the past and current treatment of Indigenous Peoples by the settler colonial nation state in Canada.

Because of this, I recommend that restorying circles with incarcerated groups contain some reflection on settler colonialism and its relationship to the epidemic of Indigenous incarceration.

Reflecting on the painful stories shared by the participants, the isolation, abuse, and poverty could lead us to assume that their trajectory from victim to offender was inevitable; that the powerlessness and pain they fought to diminish through substance abuse would ultimately lead to incarceration. However, the similarities between the loneliness and isolation in the participants' early experiences and their experiences in prison do not signify an unbreakable causal connection.

Patterns are indicative of learned responses but don't necessarily predict future behaviour or describe all that is within a person. As highlighted by the story of the eagle in the chicken pen, describing the broken eagle as a chicken does not change its core identity.

Many researchers have shown that factors such as poverty, family dysfunction, not attending school, unemployment, and drug and alcohol abuse are common among those who have been involved in criminal activity and incarcerated. While there is also research relating to reducing recidivism, resilience, and overcoming such negative factors,[48] we seldom hear the narratives of currently released Indigenous offenders who are rebuilding their lives despite traumatic histories and many years of imprisonment.

---

48 Howell, 2008; Tousignant & Sioui, 2009.

The participants in my restorying circle project are resilient, they are survivors. They have endured and overcome their past trauma related to substance abuse, violence, isolation, and an unhealthy family environment. These Indigenous participants need to continue focusing on their strength of resilience and survival and keep directing this energy toward their own healing.

The stories shared within the restorying circles told harsh truths and honoured the resilience of the participants, offering myriad glimpses of positive character traits and personal strengths. Each participant's story forced others to look at their own lives and ask, "Do I have the same resilience to overcome my struggles? Or must I continue allowing past trauma to affect my life?"

So many times, these participants were pushed to the limit, but they did not break. They survived and learned how to be tough and resilient. Seeing their own strength through their stories helped these Indigenous men. When the other men in the group reflected that strength back to them, it affirmed and enhanced their resilience. This support gave them courage and prepared them for future challenges.

Reprinting History

As a teenager, I remember being really concerned that I might develop an alcohol problem, so I tried to avoid all parties and drinking. I remember how I hated alcohol because of my childhood experiences, hence why I didn't touch it.

However, when I was eighteen, I gave in and attended a party, where I had my first experience with alcohol. Did I ever have a blast! My dopamine went through the roof. What I didn't realize was how quickly I could become addicted when I did finally try it. From that one night, the alcohol abuse I had been avoiding had taken hold of me.

And for the next three years, I abused alcohol to cover up all my past pain, right or wrong. At that time, I thought I was just enjoying myself even though I would usually end up in fights, torn t-shirts, a bloody face, and a few times picked up by the police. My saying was, "Party hard or don't party at all."

At the age of 22, I got charged with impaired driving, and I never took a drink again. It all came rushing back to me, and I committed to myself that I was going to quit. Somebody said in one of our training sessions: "something so bad, something so good." I was able to reframe and restory the way I viewed drinking alcohol.

One of my thoughts, when I was sitting in jail for the impaired charge, was that it really scared me to think of where I was heading.

An irony of this situation is that I later worked as a guard at this same jail, named "Sleepy Hollow," five years later. I also ended up working as an Indigenous cadet with the RCMP, working with the same police officer who arrested me.

He said, "Don't I know you," and I responded, "Yes, you arrested me for impaired driving a couple of years ago." We had a good laugh, and he said, "Well, you really turned your life around!"

I share my story for people to learn from my mistakes and to provide examples of how they can look at restorying their own stories. Also, to have a better understanding of how one's negative upbringing due to the effects of residential school leads to intergenerational trauma. I wish I had known a better way to deal with all of my anger caused by my unhealthy and chaotic childhood and upbringing.

My story is meant to provide others with an awareness of someone who has travelled a path of unhealthiness and negativity caused by intergenerational trauma as a result of a parent(s) attending residential school. These experiences could lead an individual to subconsciously interact with others in a negative manner and, more importantly, impact their ability to trust. Similar to my story, it is nothing that other individuals have done that defines how the Indigenous person reacts to them. However, their understanding could improve this interaction.

Every little piece of awareness that improves the understanding of the Indigenous situation and provides for intergenerational healing will only make it better.

Circles of Community

" *Because a lot of the time, I felt that no one else had been through the same crap as me. But I learned there are others like me. But each time I told what happened to me, it got a little easier. It didn't hurt so much. And were it not for storytelling, talking to people, that's what we do every day of our lives, we tell stories. I just know that I lived that story. And I'm here today because of that story, because of my story. If one person stays out as a result of hearing what I have to say, it's a good thing. Sharing. Grateful to be here to hear the stories. And I just remind myself every day that I've got to be good to myself, be happy with myself, to love myself. Try to make someone smile today. If I do that, I've succeeded in what I want to do. Meegwetch."*
—Workshop Participant

Traditionally, talking circles have five to ten participants. The restorying circle for my PhD project incorporated seven: the four participants, the Elders, the research assistant and myself. The main goal of the restorying circles was to make use of the experiences, views, and stories shared by the participants to shed new light on (and perhaps even arm them with) a potentially more positive self-formation that might foster growth and healing.

For many of the participants, the first step to combating the sense of isolation was to open up about long-buried experiences and feelings. By keeping their experiences trapped within themselves, the men had, unsurprisingly, felt those negative feelings worsen. Traumatic experiences common to Indigenous Peoples grappling with ongoing colonization and generations of cultural genocide often persisted within the unspoken territory of silent memories; such experiences served to fragment the men's self-perceptions. The restorying circles provided these men with opportunities to open up about difficult memories within the context of community support.

The restorying circles offered participants opportunities to express their stories, feelings, and thoughts, and to claim agency over the narrative arc of their life experiences—in some cases for the first time. Participants no longer needed to exist in isolation and silence, but rather became integral parts of a community based on reciprocity and sharing. Listening to other participants' stories gave the men the strength and courage to open up about their own previously hidden issues. David shared,

Coming to the circles helps me. As everybody shared, and I shared, it helps me reflect on where I've been in life. There are always things I learn from listening to

other people. I know that I'm not the only person who had a lot of problems in life."

The organization of the restorying circles enabled participants to engage in group discussion in a manner informed by Indigenous spiritual and transformative practices. Indigenous spirituality isn't described as a "religion" but as a way of healing and living. For most participants, spirituality and cultural connection are very important.

The Elders' participation added to the cultural/spiritual component of the circles which assisted the participants to stay connected to, or to reconnect with, their culture more effectively. The Elders opened and closed each restorying circle with a smudge and prayer. They acted as collaborators, facilitating a focus on healing and growth and contributing to the discussion when they thought it would be beneficial. Because the perspectives of all involved in a circle are inherently valued in Indigenous contexts, all those in the room were permitted to enter the dialogue. Laine said,

" *Coming to the circles helps me stay balanced. I try to follow and stay on a good path, to live a good life, and smudging every morning helps me. It's how I begin my day, with a prayer."*

While one participant voiced his skepticism about the existence of a higher power, arguing that only he could control his own destiny, the men collectively expressed their appreciation for the cultural and communal safety ensured by the presence of the spiritual advisor/Elder and the comfortable setting of the Four Directions Aboriginal Students' Centre. This sense of safety and collective purpose encouraged the men to allow themselves to be vulnerable and to share experiences that they had hitherto kept locked away.

The cumulative nature of the sharing within the circles proved extremely important to the participants. That the participants revealed more in successive circles was an indicator that they were building a sense of belonging and trust that allowed them to feel less isolated over time. Talking circles have been shown to enable those who had previously been forced into silence to speak and express their feelings and thoughts, perhaps for the first time.[49]

Many participants expressed feelings of empowerment through sharing their personal issues and stories, and the acceptance of needed support and advice from the other participants. Because the men tended to share experiences to which others could relate, moments of embarrassment or even shame proved extremely rare within the circles. Peter commented,

> *And that's where I learned I can do that today: I can say what happened to me. I still have some apprehension about some of the things I say because I've not told that*

---

49 Waldram, 1997, p. 136.

to many people. But I'm not ashamed of it. I just know that I lived that story. And I'm here today because of that story, because of my story."

The restorying circles gave these men, affected by the criminal justice system, a community that cared and dedicated time to address their issues through Indigenous storytelling practices. This confirms Lalonde's contention that many Indigenous males relate to a narrative rather than an essentialist identity.[50] As Krech says, "Talking circles and storytelling...and community-based spiritual ceremony have begun to find inroads into the process of 're-storying' one's life, thereby bringing about a reframed sense of 'self'."[51]

Unfortunately, for many Indigenous males involved with the criminal justice system—including the participants in this research study—negative early life experiences are often compounded by the hypermasculine identities encouraged by the prison environment. The stereotypical hypermasculine male offender within the prison system can be described as tough, street-smart, cunning, angry, deceitful, intimidating, stubborn, selfish, thoughtless, and uncaring.

Although many of the characteristics associated with hypermasculinity are negative, many inmates work hard to build these characteristics on the inside of the prison. They

---

50 Tousignant & Sioui, 2009, p. 48.
51 Krech, 2002, p.90.

do this out of the need for survival and to gain respect from fellow inmates. A prisoner learns quickly how a man should act, talk, and walk.

He gains a clear understanding of the prison hierarchy and finds his place within that hierarchy, by choice or default.[52] Inmates are taught that presenting a hypermasculine public façade is necessary, even though it may conflict with their self-identity. Various metaphors are used, such as *mask* or *armour*, to emphasize a separation between public and private identity. The armour or mask is designed to protect the inmate from revealing vulnerabilities, weaknesses, and other qualities that might undermine a hypermasculine identity.[53] One must learn the inmate code or suffer the consequences. As Deena Rymhs indicates, "In prison you must quickly learn how to slip and slide, as to survive the game of prison."[54] Sabo, Kupers, and London describe the prison "game" and the "masks" required to succeed with it as follows:

> *Suffer in silence. Never admit you are afraid...Do not snitch...do not do anything that will make other prisoners think you are gay, effeminate, or a sissy. Act hard...Do not help the authorities in any way. Do not trust anyone. Always be ready to fight, especially when your manhood*

---

52 Rymhs, 2008, p. 45.
53 Karp, 2010, p. 66.
54 Rymhs, 2008, p.24.

is challenged...One way to avoid a fight is to look as though you are willing to fight. As a result, prisoners lift weights compulsively, adopt the meanest stare they can muster, and keep their fears and their pain carefully hidden beneath a well rehearsed tough-guy posture."[55]

As I mentioned before, specific cultural programs, Elder Services, spiritual ceremonies, consultations with Indigenous staff, and other cultural healing programs encourage participants to take off the hypermasculine armour to find culturally appropriate, pro-social demonstrations of masculinity. According to Woolner:

" *Re-storying also means creating spaces in which Aboriginal peoples can re-claim their voice—and agency—and begin to put together the pieces of a fragmented, broken and silenced past, and in so doing to transform stories of victimhood into stories of resiliency, in order heal inter-generationally-sustained and transmitted traumas. In what follows, I give an overview, roughly chronological, of a number of processes—political, social, legal, and otherwise—that have emerged as spaces and processes in which this "re-storying" has begun to take place."*[56]

---

55 Sabo, Kupers & London, 2001, p. 10-11.
56 2009, section Accounting for Narrative in Peacebuilding, para. 2.

This is relevant because people may need time to revisit and share their past traumas. Individuals sometimes bury their deepest emotions/secrets, and it can take time to speak about them. The fear of people's traumatic experiences can become diminished as they are shared repeatedly.

During each of our circles, an eagle feather was passed, and each person was given an opportunity to speak. While I recommended areas for reflection each session, participants could pass if they wished, and they could speak on any topic that suited them for as long as they wanted. An objective of the restorying circles was for participants to recognize that others were dealing with similar difficulties and that they were not alone with their issues.

Participating in the restorying circles changed the attitudes that perpetuate the myth that "I belong in prison." Uncovering some of the core issues that influenced these participants' paths to involvement with the criminal justice system could create conditions where participants might walk a different, healing journey. Sharing stories can bring repressed trauma into the light and allow the renewal to begin. Restorying within a community with others with similar backgrounds and with the support of culturally knowledgeable Elders can facilitate awareness and rebuilding identities.

Indigenous scholar Russell Bishop speaks of how important it is for community members to share their own stories.[57] He states that "story telling is a useful and culturally appropriate way of representing the 'diversities of truth' within which the storyteller rather than I retains control."[58] Meseyton states that the healing journey typically involves several key steps.[59] First, it involves identifying areas of change. Then, individuals tell one's stories, allowing space for a new Indigenous identity to emerge. Next, they analyze the trauma and how it links to unhealthy behaviour. Lastly, creating a new vision of self where individual healing is part of community healing.

It's crucial to note that the story-sharing process allowed my PhD research participants to explore and reflect with others who had similar experiences growing up and being incarcerated. Although these stories don't necessarily indicate that each participant's beliefs about himself have transformed, I feel that by hearing each other's stories and their visions for a good future, all participants had the opportunity to build personal hope.

The participants' continued attendance and their increased willingness to share freely and reveal deeper emotions over time indicated that the restorying circles were perceived as valuable—even if a comparative analysis

---

57 Bishop, 1999.
58 As cited in Wesley-Esquimaux & Calliou, 2010, p. 26.
59 Meseyton, 2005.

of initial stories with later stories would not reveal a sub-
stantive metamorphosis.

One potential reason for this failure of the hypothesis
is that at the time of our initial circle, all of the participants
could be described as being on their healing journeys, even
as their stories revealed they were at different stages and
on unique trajectories. Another reason may be that it just
takes much longer (weeks, months, or even years) to witness
changes. Some participants could even be said to have already
begun the restorying process, while others were at earlier
stages of self-awareness.

David looked back on the all-consuming nature of the
difficulties he had experienced in the past, thinking through
his own capacity to make change. He reflected:

> ❝ *Maybe I've got too many problems, and I couldn't
> stop. And I was angry at myself for not listening to my
> parents. It is hard to find what my problem is. I didn't
> hurt because I was too young. I've been holding that in
> a long time, I haven't told anyone that. But sometimes
> I was hiding and crying about that. I did that a lot,
> hiding and crying...So many years I'd been like that, I
> don't care. And it was hard to find people to talk, only
> when I'm drunk, and then I start talking. My past, it
> was not good because I was drunk sometimes, and I lie a
> lot. I was lying all the time. So many years I was doing
> that. I'm getting happier. I'm getting more open, more
> honest. I didn't kill any people, I was taking programs,*

*but I wasn't listening, but I didn't take it seriously. I
didn't have any problem like that but today I'm happy
now. I'm going to do this more and more (attending
circles), getting more interested, more talking, more open
(about his feelings), honest, so…I want to feel better now."*

Even as he acknowledged the overwhelming nature of
influences beyond his control and recognized the difficulty
of unearthing struggles within the self, David registered by
the end of his remarks his dedication to change: "I'm going
to do this more and more, getting more interested, more talk,
more open, honest so…I want to feel better now."

The active nature of this final statement is crucial, identifying what the participant is going to do and mobilizing
the agency he retains to be more "open" and "honest." David
acknowledges that many hurts were kept inside and dulled
by drugs or alcohol. This often kept him from seeing the
results of his own behaviour on those around him. It seemed
that he repeated these stories in subsequent circles, but
restorying often involves multiple retellings before change
can be solidified.[60]

The circles offered David a chance to listen to and learn
from the stories of others and to begin to face his own history.

As we shared experiences, the participants' stories reflected changing perceptions and attitudes from one session

---

60 Tousignant & Sioui, 2009, p. 48-49.

to the next. David's reiteration of the same stories multiple times but with slight variations concurs with Tousignant's thesis that restorying often requires multiple retellings to allow individuals to create new understandings of their identities. As David shared, he desired to move forward in a healthy way. From working with Indigenous people involved in the justice system over many years, I have witnessed this phenomenon repeatedly.

Some worry that participants could re-victimize themselves by reflecting on and revisiting the negative issues in the past. Perhaps they're taking a step in the wrong direction and not moving forward in their healing journey. Sometimes, even the listeners' reactions end up locking those sharing their stories into a victim mentality.

Recently, the Truth and Reconciliation forums have publicly shared the shameful practices of the residential school system and the *Indian Act*, which has served to suppress, oppress, and victimize Indigenous Peoples in Canada. Canada's history of colonization and dealing with the "Indian problem" through avenues of cultural genocide and assimilation has silenced and taken power away from Indigenous Peoples. These atrocities have negatively impacted future generations of Indigenous children through intergenerational trauma.

However, Indigenous individuals often do realize that our feelings of inferiority and incapability have been created and imposed on us by the colonial powers and that we have a richer cultural history than we have been provided with by Canadian society.

It was crucial throughout the restorying process to ensure that the men engaged with their histories in ways that didn't just rehearse the negative stories that colonialism invented about Indigenous Peoples. Rather than being a liberating experience, such disclosures can reinforce shame and entrench negative identities. As such, the restorying process was repeatedly affirmed to be strengths-based, as evidenced by Peter's resiliency.

Peter had begun sharing his story with various groups and Indigenous communities before the advent of the restorying circles. As such, he would be considered well into the restorying process. For example, he shared with the group:

> *I have a strong will, I came to realize. Rarely did I complain about treatment or conditions, which surrounded us. I endured much that would have broken, I guess, many. I recall telling some of my early life experiences, up to the time of incarceration, to my unit while I was at the Northern Treatment Centre in Sault Ste. Marie. And upon completion of this narration, my counsellor's first remark was, "I don't know why you didn't hang yourself." What kind of response was that?! Up to then, I thought my experience was normal because, for me it was, it was real, and I had lived it."*

Peter demonstrated to the rest of the community the importance of engaging with difficult past experiences through story, and here, he modeled a restorying principle of identifying strengths within the self that others might not acknowledge (even within the context of personal hardship and trauma). With this particular story, he demonstrated the importance of a supportive and culturally aware audience to share personal history safely.

All the participants struggled, suffered, endured, and showed the true meaning of resilience, by surviving their past traumatic events within often dysfunctional families and throughout lengthy incarcerations at various provincial and federal prisons. They brought this strength to our circles, but they also brought their compassion and support.

When Laine shared how his feelings toward his dad changed from white to grey to black, that disillusionment coloured his perceptions, isolating him further from his dad and maybe others. However, when he saw himself using similar violence in relationships, he may have been able to understand the connections between the historical disempowerment of Indigenous Peoples and his own and his father's recourse to violence. He may even have been able to forgive his dad and himself.

This potential revelation may not have been possible without the support and guidance of the other participants within the restorying circle. Even though these participants were "hardened criminals," they still could show acts of kindness, understanding, and love to their family/community members and one another within the restorying circles.

Early during the restorying circle project, if the participants noticed another participant struggling to share past traumatic events, words of support and encouragement appeared, which perhaps assisted the participants by assuring them that they were not alone. The participants could feel their peers' pain and sorrow, but more importantly, they could hear the hope and aspiration.

This was evidenced by the participants' words of support, which gave each other the courage to remember, share, better understand, and live with their past experiences in increasingly healthy ways. Peter's story above about the Northern Treatment Centre in Sault Ste. Marie illuminates the kind of toxic storytelling environment that the restorying circles were designed to avoid, and it drives home the necessity of reciprocal care within the community of storytellers.

The restorying process opens up opportunities for reflection and revisiting and revising stories within a caring community, where others listen without judgment or surprise. In such an environment, the men are encouraged to recognize that they're not solely responsible for the negative experiences that have befallen them and that they do carry the potential for growth and change.

They are also encouraged to take pride in their perseverance and survival, and to further acknowledge, reflect upon, and renew the strengths and positive attributes within themselves. It's important to realize that participants' problems were not simply eliminated once they identified them within their stories; however, their personal and collective recognition of their capacity to face those problems over the long term proved inspiring.

As Peter remarked:

> *I did not like myself for years. I tattooed my body to make myself less attractive to the world I was in. It didn't have the effect I looked for. I abused my mind and soul with drugs to forget, but the memories are just as alive today as if I lived them yesterday. But with proper nourishment, they do not hurt as much and some cases, they do not hurt at all even though they scarred me for decades. The healing is slow and does not come overnight. Flashbacks and triggers happened over a few years ago, especially about the sexual abuse. For more than a year, I was triggered by smells, sounds, and sights, and I would break down completely out of nowhere. I'm fortunate that I have a loving and caring partner who helped me through these difficult periods."*

Listening to other participants' stories aided some of the men in their own restorying processes. This was evidenced repeatedly as participants referred to each other's narratives when sharing their own stories. Making these connections may have given them insight into their experiences and created opportunities to share long-buried memories. For example, Laine referenced another's story of putting a pillow over his head to help drown out the sounds of violence in the home:

> *I saw a lot of violence when I was a child. I didn't like it. Especially when it was toward my mother. I saw my father hitting my mother for the first time as a young boy. I wanted to grab something and try to defend her but there was nothing for me to grab because I was a young boy and I didn't know what to do. All I could do was run for cover for myself, and when you were talking about the pillow over your head, that brought back a lot of memories because that's what I used to do as a child."*

In our final session, he shared along similar lines:

> *But from what I remember about my childhood growing up, I used to hide whenever I'd hear the adults partying, because eventually they'd be fighting. I'd always put the pillow over my head and just scream or block it all out because I didn't want to hear the violence, the drinking and stuff. I find myself still doing that today just to block out certain things and just to fall asleep. It may be a negative thing from the past, but it's also a positive thing I find because it helps me fall asleep*

at night and whenever I can't calm down in my own thoughts sometimes."

Like Peter, Laine acknowledges the return of traumatic memories unbidden in a way that many listeners might perceive as debilitating; he said, after all, that "it may be a negative thing." Yet he highlighted the agency he retains and, therefore, his power over the return of his past. He reclaimed the act of placing a pillow over his head as something other than ongoing victimization: "It's also a *positive* thing because it helps me fall asleep at night."

In an earlier session Laine had shared that he couldn't remember his early years, but connecting with the story shared by another triggered memories he thought he did not possess. Facing the violence and the fear allowed for an interpretation of his actions and responses throughout his life.

Laine was also extremely forthright about his institutionalization and his perpetuation of learned violent behaviours within and beyond the household. He articulated:

66 *Then I started getting stuck in the federal system. I didn't realize how fast my life was changing. Being stuck in the federal system and the next thing you know, time is going on, it's like where'd my twenties go, where'd my thirties go, I lost it all. Like I explained before, I never had a job until I was 32 years old. I never made an honest living until then. It's the same thing with relationships; they were always just short, limited.*

They were always filled with drugs and alcohol, which always led to violence. I guess I've always told myself that there were things in my life that I would never want to see done to, well, when I've seen my father do that to a woman and I've done that, you know, I've been charged with domestic violence, and I asked an Elder about this before and well it's things that you see when you're young is what you learn right? I didn't want to turn out to be that way, but eventually, I ended up getting into trouble like that."

Like the other members of the group, Laine's stories revealed how the pain, abuse, and violence of family members and others impacted his own childhood, and how he continued to live with pain and anger and even perpetuated that violence upon others, thus highlighting the nature of intergenerational trauma.

Although there was little evidence of participants changing their stories in significant ways throughout these sessions, there was meaningful participation by all involved. Powerful words were gifted to the circle with sensitivity and received gratefully by its members. Some of the participants appeared to have already done a good deal of restorying work, and multiple members expressed a desire to continue doing restorying work beyond the purview of my PhD project to help themselves and others.

Peter shared how he has been using his experiences to share with, listen to, and support others within the Indigenous community:

" *Now that I'm a little older, I know I have a responsibility to help the youth through their experiences. I can share my story with them and hope they can learn something. I can empathize with them and how they feel—the loneliness, despair, and the reasons for using drugs or alcohol."*

Laine indicated to the group that he recognized that he had become a man he didn't want to be, but more importantly, that he finally has realized that he can live a different story:

" *Today, I choose not to use drugs or alcohol because of the way I felt. That's not me; I don't like feeling that way. Today, I like to be the person that people look at me in a good way, instead of that bad, negative way. I don't want to be known as the person stuck in the system all my life. Drugs and alcohol were quite the bad experience for me: I've overdosed a couple of times, and I thank my blessings every day that I came back. My mother is always telling me there's a reason for you to come back here; it's not your time yet. You got to change. And that's what I do every day. I try to be the better person that I can be."*

Healing can often be aided by the opportunity to share one's life story with calmness when previously it was interrupted by chaos and negative emotions. To that end, these circles created a safe space for listening and sharing painful stories without shame in a supportive environment. These circles not only inspired those directly involved but also offered valuable insights for others seeking to reclaim their own stories.

The courage, generosity, vulnerability, and care of these men, in their interactions with each other in the circle, generated opportunities for them all to affirm identities beyond those imposed upon them by colonial history and by the hypermasculinity conditioned within the prison—opportunities to strengthen their eagle wings, to soar above the negative life experiences, and to envision positive ways and culturally aware means of living moving forward.

As the next chapter explores, the concept of restorying one's story is applicable to everyone, regardless of background or experience. By creating safe spaces for sharing and listening, we can facilitate a journey toward self-discovery, healing, and a more positive future.

You Can Restory
Your Story, Too

I believe that restorying works, and it will help people who are willing to give it a try. It's an opportunity to feel better and more balanced when it comes to one's spiritual, emotional, mental, and physical well-being. Everyone has tragedy; everyone has pain. This isn't dependent on social status, gender, or culture—everyone, to some degree, suffers. For Indigenous people, we have already discussed many of the root causes for the diversion of people's stories. Now our task is to help them restory their story.

One of the ways to begin restorying your story is to want to change and become on better terms with your past. Meaning that you need the motivation to want to turn down the volume of your past traumatic story that continues to play loudly in your head. This old story may drive your own choices and way of living.

I also believe attending a cultural event or ceremony that is offered in the community you are living in will begin you on your healing path. The very first step you can take toward restorying your life story is the willingness to open up and release the demons from the closet. If you really want to restory your story, you have to shine a light on the unhealthy narrative that keeps you in the dark.

The next step is to write down your story onto the Medicine Wheel Tipi model. This can be in paragraphs, bullet points, minimal adjectives, or even pictures. You can refer to the exercises in the back of the book to make your own Medicine Wheel Tipi.

Sometimes, people who are really struggling cannot, or will not, be able to write down their past trauma on paper but are willing to verbally share some of their traumatic stories, and you can choose this route, too. You need to be able to open up and share in a healthy and culturally friendly environment, ideally in a communal setting, such as a talking circle or restorying circle where the others present can relate and have walked a similar path as you. After sharing, it is important to listen and really hear what the other people are saying about their stories. What you hear can make you feel like you are not the only one suffering.

The next step, which is sometimes the most difficult, is to look at your past story and revisit, recuperate, and restory this story into a healthier version that works for you today.

The final step is to share your "restoried" personal story with others. Again, the healing process of doing so is tremendous, as one of the key factors is that you listen and possibly learn from others how they have overcome or continue to manage their past traumatic story in a healthier manner.

Restorying Your Story is a lifelong journey that requires courage.

However, sharing and talking about your story in a healing manner can lead to reclaiming, restoring, and reconnecting to your self, family, and community.

Participants at a different facilitated session with frontline workers in Ontario saw restorying as "a tool to allow people to open up" and "re-frame their experiences and lighten their burdens from their life experiences." They were excited to implement it with the people they support. In our sessions, we share the following quote:

> " *In the Indigenous worldview, healing is a lifelong process following the same spiralling pattern as an eagle in flight: the eagle soars higher and higher by spiralling upwards in ever-widening circles. This pattern of flight teaches that healing also progresses cyclically, each new stage offering deeper insights as preparation for the next."*

When it comes to facilitation, we want to symbolize a positive shift, envisioning the unhealthy past being overtaken by a healthy present and future. Understanding the past is crucial for moving forward. We create healthier words or phrases for each side of the tipi to represent our journey.

This has helped us facilitate sessions with large groups, like a session with more than twenty participants from the staff at Thunder Woman Healing Lodge in Toronto, who felt a sense of openness, that they were guided and comfortable sharing in a big circle, and that they had gone on an unexpected journey. They identified their strengths, like perseverance, optimism, empathy, and bravery. By the end of the session, we designed a personalized tool they can carry with them, a symbol of their growth and transformation that will continue to evolve as they embark on this new path.

Some of the participants in the same session were able to recognize that even "the smallest step in the right direction can change the entire path (system)."

Importance of Spirituality and Culture

" Coming to the circles helps me stay balanced, I guess. I try to follow and stay on a good path, to live a good life, and smudging every morning helps me. It's how I begin my day with a prayer. Whereas in the past, I didn't bother, I didn't care. That's how I just keep living my good life. That's what I try to do every day. I don't want to go back to where I was before. Coming in circles like this helps me a lot. I'm very thankful to you guys for sharing your stories, I'm very thankful for that. I learned a lot."

— Workshop Participant

Many researchers have acknowledged that Indigenous spirituality and culture are vital for healing. This healing benefits individuals, families, and communities. The criminal justice system has addressed this by providing Elders and cultural and spiritual programs for prison inmates. Many inmates have found these programs invaluable in helping them heal, develop healthy personal identities, and find a supportive community.

Most participants in the restorying circles related to my PhD project articulated connections with culture and spirituality when sharing the stories of their early lives.

Ryan shared, "My dad had taught me who I was, the Mohawk nation, and that we have a certain way of doing things." One of the ways he described was that "we don't stand up for *God Save the Queen*, we don't stand up for *The Lord's Prayer*, those aren't our ways." Ryan's dad talked about the Creator and following a certain traditional way.

"As I grew up, I tried to connect to the ideal of the Creator, but I never found that connection. The only time when I was young that I felt a connection to anything was when I was by myself in the bush."

His father was highly traditional, but the integration between traditional teachings and the broader socialization through mainstream education and dominant Christianity created tensions for Ryan as a young person:

> " *Now, even though the old man tried to teach me about the Creator, the directions and everything else, he still allowed me to go to church. I walked away from that pretty quick after I figured out what was going on there. There was a lot of hypocrisy.*"

Such hypocrisy negatively impacted Ryan's experiences with spirituality and culture. He described, for example, being forced by his father to become someone he wasn't. As a young child, he was confused because his father told him it was okay to be Indigenous. Then he was being punished at school for expressing his Indigenous identity.

"Unfortunately, going into school, I found a lot of conflicts with it, with teachers and that school in particular had a principal that used to run a residential school, or was part of a residential school."

His experiences in his community caused further confusion regarding his identity. He explained,

> *I didn't suffer from racism from white people, but I suffered racism from Native people because, at the time, being Native down there wasn't the thing. You weren't supposed to know who you were; you weren't supposed to accept the idea that you're supposed to be Indian."*

He experienced confusion, hypocrisy, and little guidance in terms of cultural teachings and their relevance. It's little surprise, therefore, that he has apprehension and negative feelings toward spirituality and the Creator. Ryan shared:

> *I'm not a spiritual person. I say I'm not a spiritual person because, in a sense, I don't believe in a Creator. I don't believe in God. I don't believe in a higher power. I believe in myself. All my life, somebody has defined what I'm supposed to be. And I finally realized if I'm going to follow who I am, if I follow what I think is true in my heart, I can't believe in somebody else to help me, I have to help myself."*

Peter, who comes from a long line of Iroquoian people and is very connected to Indigenous spiritual practices himself, responded to some of Ryan's statements with support, seeking common ground.

"People don't have to believe in the Creator anytime either," Peter said. "There were years when I didn't want to believe in that. But to believe in something, even if it is yourself, is a good thing."

Although the teachings he received were inconsistent and complicated by tensions within the community, Ryan had the advantage of more opportunities to learn about his culture growing up than most of the other participants, who seldom had positive experiences related to cultural connection and spirituality. Peter and Laine both discovered their spirituality inside the prison system.

Laine explained:

    " I knew who I was as a person, as a young Native person, but I wasn't brought up with the teachings. My first teachings I remember as a young person, I was in the [youth centre]. That's when I started learning about our traditional ways, but I didn't want to disrespect the medicines because every time I got released, I got back into drugs or alcohol, and I didn't want to bring that around the medicines."

Peter concurred, stating, "I was on the fence from time to time from using drugs and alcohol, but I never mixed this with going to ceremonies. I just stayed away spiritually and never mix drugs and ceremonies."

Peter and Laine agreed that the most profound healing they experienced while in correctional facilities came from Indigenous spiritual practices rather than through Eurocentric counselling programs. Laine agreed with something Peter had spoken about earlier: "As I heard earlier, I got more out of a sweat lodge than a six-month program. I learned more about myself in that sweat lodge than what I did with any other program."

While Ryan stressed that he did not view himself as a spiritual person, he conceded within the circle: "I don't mind coming to [cultural ceremonies]. I like the smell of the sage, sweet grass, the smell of the incense burning. I like to hear other people talk. I like listening to their stories, and I like hearing the sincerity." Like Peter, Ryan was willing to honour and respect the particular beliefs of others in the circle even as they did not align with his own. This commitment to openness and supporting others along their divergent pathways of healing greatly enhanced the atmosphere of safety and reciprocity within the restorying circles.

Peter and Laine each referenced being given Indigenous spirit names, which impacted and shaped their identities. Peter spoke about this, saying that his spirit name was "given to me by the Lakota people, and it means 'One Cast Aside.'"

Laine described being given his spirit name, which means "Morning Sky." He continued, saying the man who gifted him the name "blew my mind, just the way he came about my

Indian name because as a child I remember I always used to look up at the sky and here's this man, forty years later, telling me something I reflected on to help me get through the day, that time of the morning."

Peter and Laine both agreed that spirituality and culture are important to their daily living and that attending group cultural events like these circles is important to their healing. Peter said,

> The traditional teachings gave me an ideal foundation of how I wanted to live, and I earnestly believe this was possible once released. I work with Elders, go to ceremonies, and do one-on-ones with people when I have to. And I believe strongly in our traditions. Prior to coming in contact with the prison system, I wouldn't have said that."

Laine shared, in a similar vein,

> That's why I turned to our medicines every morning just to help me get through the day. Coming to the circles helps me stay balanced, I guess. I try to follow and stay on a good path, to live a good life, and smudging every morning helps me. It's how I begin my day with a prayer. Whereas in the past, I didn't bother, I didn't care."

Another aspect of spiritual practice that was mobilized during the restorying circles was the act of holding an eagle feather during particular sessions while participants shared their stories. Peter described the relationship between the feather and the strength to speak the truth: "I asked for the feather because when we talk with the feather, it means that we have to speak our truth."

However, Ryan expressed concern that people don't actually want to hear the truth in circles like the one in which we were participating. He explained, "I guess when I get in the circles mostly, and I get talking about stuff, I realize that not a lot of people want to hear the truth."

Ryan indicated that in such spaces, he felt that people did not genuinely listen to him, whether or not he spoke the truth. He likened this to his teenage years, when he felt that his interactions with others often acted as wallpaper covering a mouldy structure underneath: "I'd do something, get people laughing but basically nothing, there was no substance there, no truth to it."

In the past, Ryan did not trust others' reactions to him or his stories because he was only acting, not sharing his true self, as he felt there was no substance in previous sharing places. His story about his relationship with his family, especially his father, directly impacted how he viewed others. He had a tremendous distrust of people's sincerity because he was always the one getting hurt or turned away as a child.

The pain and suffering he went through growing up relates to the mouldy structure of his relationships, and the wallpaper speaks to people acting like they care when, to him, they don't really care. Just as the wallpaper only covers up but does not eliminate the mould underneath, Ryan worried that people's feigned concern will never eliminate their ill intentions.

Profound skepticism regarding the motivations and sincerity of participants and organizers informed Ryan's ambivalence toward cultural ceremonies: "I have for years stayed away from ceremonies, I've stayed away from smudging, and I've stayed away from a lot of things when it gets into a group gathering." Ryan connected to his spirituality by spending time on bike trails and alone in the bush rather than in organized spiritual settings.

"I get out into the trail," he explained. "That's where I feel my peace, my comfort, where I feel my spirituality. It's where I'm at my happiest, where I feel my most free. It's the place I feel I belong."

As such, for Ryan to attend all of the restorying circles was a difficult challenge, and one from which he described gleaning potential benefits:

" *So overall, I understand the reason for the groups, I understand why they're put together, and they get the circles going because guys need it. Maybe I need it in a way at times, get me thinking again about things. Maybe get me talking about things I don't talk about enough. But in general, I did enjoy listening to what people had to say. There are mirrors in my life, there are things that I thought about that I could have said that was already said with their stories."*

All PhD research participants mentioned connecting in some way with Indigenous culture within the prison system. Many Indigenous men have not been presented with cultural and spiritual teachings until their involvement in the prison system because of the legislated suppression of Indigenous ways of knowing throughout the centuries of settler colonialism. Some of the participants grew up largely in non-Indigenous foster homes, and some grew up in homes where those who practised Indigenous spirituality were also negative influences in other ways. As such, most of the men were unaware of many of their cultural practices before entering prison.

Unfortunately, in prison, the hope and healing offered by cultural programs is often negated when the men return to the cell block and need to put back on the hypermasculine exterior required to survive within the institution. Those teachings, and the spiritual and cultural connections they have just experienced, get suffocated by the toxic prison environment.

The valuable element about the reconnection and introduction to one's culture is that it begins a process for the men, answering crucial questions regarding their identities and how the teachings might assist with rediscovering and restorying who they are as Indigenous people.

For three of the four participants, this cultural and spiritual connection while imprisoned ultimately sparked the beginnings of their personal reflection and the desire to retell and restory their own stories. During these moments, the participants started questioning their negative past experiences.

When finally released from prison, a major priority for most of these participants was having spirituality and cultural activities as part of their lives on the outside. Spiritual ceremonies and cultural activities were necessary to keep the participants at balance spiritually, mentally, emotionally, and physically and to keep them connected to their beliefs and values.

Before this awakening, all the men had abused substances to endure, or escape for a limited time, the hardships in their lives. Recognizing the difference between using substances to escape and using ceremonies and spirituality to face their lives is a major difference for these men: it was a matter of being released into the community or back in prison. It was much easier for the participants to choose the life they have known best, which involves substance abuse and criminality, than to strive to learn and participate in their cultures.

Yet, as they got older, they realized that this life has led them to incarceration. The participants' priority after our sessions was to seek out spiritual ceremonies and cultural activities to live in the community and grow in health and strength. Most mentioned that this supports them in leading a pro-social and law-abiding lifestyle.

Outside of the prison, however, there may be few opportunities for these men to connect with culture and receive support from programs such as this restorying project, particularly in an urban setting like Kingston. Ex-offenders are often limited in terms of where they can reside, so they may not be allowed to travel to communities or healing places to receive culturally specific support. Holding these restorying circles in this community provided much-needed opportunities for these participants to further develop the spiritual knowledge they had discovered inside the prison system to pursue further healing.

Persistence of Hope

Even though participants in restorying circles experience negative situations throughout their lives, the stories they have shared were often peppered with healthier reflections throughout our circles. In a large group session with Thunder Woman Healing Lodge's staff, participants reflected that you could use your own story to inspire healing in others and yourself, and that culture, through the Medicine Wheel, would help with the path forward.

This was somewhat counter to the expectations of my PhD project, whose hypothesis had been that the initial sharing of life experiences by Indigenous men whose lives had been impacted by the criminal justice system would tend to gravitate toward the negative, and that over time, these stories could be re-imagined to take on more positivity.

But the positive moments shared by the men created dynamic energy within the circles, and it provided participants with a shared sense of hope right from our initial meeting. For example, Peter recalled his central purpose as a younger person was to protect his brothers from their parents when they were on a drinking binge.

"On these occasions," he explained, "I would lead [my brothers] away from home, sometimes for a couple of days, until the drinking was over. These times were hard in some respects, but I managed to keep my brothers safe, which was my intention."

These moments of protection instilled in him parental skills of caring and nurturing, which he stated had taught him to be a better parent to his own sons. He also shared that he was forced to clean and accomplish certain tasks around the foster home, which he shared taught him a sense of responsibility and accountability when he began his life as a worker. Today, he takes his responsibility of working hard to take care of his family very seriously.

Even though most of the experiences that he shared about his foster family were negative—including constant and escalating physical and emotional abuse—he was able, from our inaugural meeting, to recognize some positive contributions to his character that were informed by his difficult early life.

David shared how when he was young, he learned how to hunt and survive off the land. The ability to live in the frigid cold through hunting and fishing, while supporting the survival of others, was seen as a personal accomplishment.

"Getting out on the land, I did that a lot before, so people taught me how to survive. It's very hard, it's very dangerous, especially in the wintertime."

Though he recounted how poverty and substance abuse appeared to map out his pathway in life, these stories of survival and resilience helped him express how prison was not his only destiny. He described in his early adulthood teaching others in the community to fish and to hunt, and he explained to us how he even started his own business: "I did two weeks on the land for students to teach them the land, the names, how to skin caribou, fish. I was happy. I liked it because we were with real people, and we got boats (canoes), teaching young people."

Sharing these positive aspects of caring for younger siblings and wanting to mentor and support others in the future revealed that the desire and capacity for connection with others had not been lost. Not only did David express a sense of satisfaction with these accomplishments, but he self-identified as having the knowledge and experience to serve his community and to make it stronger, irrespective of his difficult history of incarceration.

In addition to opening up about their issues and struggles, participants demonstrated a willingness within the circles to voice the need for help, which proved to be a major positive step in combating isolation. After having been in the prison system for so many years, asking for help would not seem initially to be an option for these men, as asking for help would be perceived within the prison culture as a sign of weakness. However, asking for help and opening up about personal issues could assist these men in avoiding difficulties in the future that might again involve incarceration.

Laine described having trouble remembering his younger years, but when sharing his experiences on the streets—which included committing offences to support his addictions—he was able to reflect on the lessons he had learned throughout his years in the prison system and to see alternative opportunities for himself. He stated:

> " *I'm thankful I went to prison...because it opened my eyes this time around, because I always let the drugs and the alcohol take care of [me], and this time it's [me] taking care of drugs and alcohol in the good way. Instead of fighting it, I find I don't let that stuff come into my life anymore because I know what it does to me, and I don't like being the only person, what it does to me, how I feel, how I think, and where it leads me to.*"

While incarcerated, some of the participants had been recognized for being role models for other inmates who looked up to them. This is somewhat ironic because these participants had described having few positive role models while growing up, so becoming role models themselves inside the prison system represents an unsung accomplishment. Peter shared how he was able to deal with his life sentence spent in different institutions:

> " *The other guys in the institution looked to me as a leader as far as Native politics were concerned, and I was quite often the Chairperson of each of the Native brotherhoods in each institution I was housed.*"

He also described receiving his Bachelor of Arts degree while in prison. Peter affirmed:

" *I've been working with the same company for almost seven years now and have established a place in the Native community in [two major Canadian cities]."*

Persevering in this fashion after having been incarcerated for much of his life, having had few positive role models, and having dealt with his own victimization as a child—while simultaneously dealing with the shame and hurt that came with the offences he committed toward his victims—speaks to Peter's capacity for resilience and survival. His story and current life show evidence of his restorying. His participation in my PhD project was a stimulus and encouragement for the rest of us.

In training sessions with the Mi'kmaw Legal Support Network staff members, we looked at the past pain/trauma of their clients, the negative story we might tell ourselves about this, and then we looked at a healthier way to restory it. This was all toward building the resilience of their clients. When they restoried, they knew they needed to really focus on using the language of care and compassion when dealing with past pain like trauma, lack of trust, and racism. They learned to take the time needed to build trust, and identified cultural elements like learning Indigenous languages from an Elder as a healthy way forward for their clients.

All of the participants in the restorying circles from my PhD research would be considered resilient because they're all trying to have a good life now despite the preponderance of extremely challenging negative past experiences. To many people, their lives may not appear to display positive accomplishments, but for these participants, survival and hope are major achievements. Peter suggested,

> *"I never did like accepting compliments for positive acts, probably because it was absent while growing up. But now I'm getting used to it, but that's something else. At least I can recognize when I've accomplished something I'm proud of."*

The men in the circle recognized the difficulty and the long-term commitment required for healing processes, but they were careful to illuminate the strengths they had displayed in their journeys toward these goals. This balance between genuine acknowledgement of ongoing difficulties—both systemic and interpersonal—and commitment to recognizing personal strengths and accomplishments bodes well for the men moving forward.

Once personal healing begins, one's eyes are often open to opportunities to help others trapped in negative situations. Some participants mentioned how they would like to give back and speak with youth in their communities. Peter shared:

> *Now that I'm a little older, I know I have a responsibility to help the youth through their experiences...I will not*

judge them; I can listen and will listen. I may not have
solutions much of the time, but we share common prob-
lems. I can only tell them how I worked through them."

Reconnection to family, community, culture, nature, and
spirituality is the main way for Indigenous people to heal,
as confirmed by McCormick.[61] This connection was missing
in the participants' young lives. The volunteering that some
of the men were involved in showed that they were being
accepted by society instead of further excluded.

These participants' stories throughout the restorying
circles have not demonstrated miraculous changes, but many
factors have combined to suggest that they are moving in the
right direction. Howell identifies nine categories for living a
crime-free life. These factors include staying sober, opening
up to spirituality and cultural connection, recognizing positive
personal identity, attaining and keeping employment, and
attending culturally informed healing groups like the restorying circles.[62] By combining these factors, the participants
are actively turning their lives around.

Some of these factors have influenced different participants more than others, but their stories share a growing
positive sense of personal identity. Such cultural tools
enabled the participants to restore, build, and strengthen

---

61   McCormick, 1994.
62   Howell, 2008, p. ii.

their identities as Indigenous men. They came to know themselves as an important and valued community member, and developed a sense of belonging within a network of care.

Sharing Your Past for Present Strength

Restorying circles provide opportunities to remember and share positive past experiences which lead participants to think of their strengths and be hopeful for the future. This enabled them to restory their current situation with positive self-messaging, such as "I am not alone, people do care for and love me, there are positive role models, and I want to be a better father, son, family member, and person."

There was one circle per week, and at the end of each circle, the participants were advised what the discussion for the next week would be. This provided the participants with the opportunity to take their time to think about their past stories and experiences, and decide in their own manner how to share about their past for the next week. This progressive structure enabled participants to revise and restory their own stories to make them relevant to the guided discussion and to consider what to share and what to keep from others in the circle.

Giving Back

Finding avenues for service to the community could provide new stories for these Indigenous men to create, share, and live. Many of the participants proved passionate about their desire to give back to their communities by speaking to youth and directing them on a good path. These participants could be positive role models to youth, sharing their life stories and experiences with Indigenous youth to help the next generation avoid getting involved with the criminal justice system in the first place.

The participants in this restorying circle project could act as guest speakers in Indigenous classrooms. They could even employ the restorying circle model as a teaching tool to assist Indigenous youth who often struggle to open up and share their stories; similarly, the Medicine Wheel Tipi could be employed as a prompt for further reflection with Indigenous youth to facilitate the restorying process. In these ways, the participants in the restorying circle project could act as role models for Indigenous youth within their communities.

As was made clear as the men shared their stories throughout the circles, the absence of positive role models in their own lives had increased their isolation and made them more susceptible to criminality; now, they desired to prevent such isolation for those who have come after them.

Being with a group of men who had suffered similar difficult and traumatic experiences as children, who had also been incarcerated, and who were now trying to lead pro-social lives, allowed them to provide possible alternative solutions for each other's personal problems. For example, Peter was a motivational speaker to youth groups in northern Indigenous communities. Peter revealed:

> " *And I'm bound to teach others through the stories. I'm invited up to James Bay to tell my story. I've never pulled the 14 hours up there, the 14 hours back. Talk to the youth up there. I know about the gang life in jail. I know what jail does to people. I know how backwards it is. And if they can stay out of it, that's a good thing. If one person stays out as a result of hearing what I have to say, it's a good thing. But if no one stays out of it, I can say that you can survive it. You can still learn good things in there.*"

These men have often been told what to do or how to fix their problems by workers who represent the authorities. To maintain their identities, they have often resisted this guidance. Having their peers provide guidance and direction may open new pathways for addressing past experiences and working in positive futures. This process of sharing, reflection, and healing allowed each individual to retell, reflect, revise, and restory as was evident in the last few sessions of the research project. Peter described:

> *I took the risk and said I want to take this week, and I'm going to say what's in my heart and what's in my mind. It's a risk, yeah. Because a lot of the time, I felt that no one else had been through the same crap as me. But I learned there are others like me. But each time I told what happened to me, it got a little easier. It didn't hurt so much. And that's where I learned I can do that today."*

According to the participants, sharing the pain and buried memories, in many cases, diminished some of the corrosive impact of past trauma and created space for hope and healing to grow. The restorying circles allowed some of these men, perhaps for the first time, to uncover past demons. Laine expressed,

"Coming to the circles helps me. As everybody shared, and I shared, it helps me reflect on where I've been in life. I know that I'm not the only person who had a lot of problems in life." In the space of the circles, I could hear and feel the participants become more open, vulnerable, and honest, which suggests some form of transformation. Ryan supported this assessment, saying, "Overall, I didn't mind coming here. I enjoyed the ride, I enjoyed the ride leaving, I enjoyed the talk." Previously, he was against attending and participating in any spiritual ceremonies for several years because of people's disrespect toward one another. Ryan stated:

❝ I've seen too often people doing that and then just walk away with meanness in their heart for that person. I have for years stayed away from ceremonies, I've stayed away from smudging, I've stayed away from a lot of things when it gets into a group gathering."

However, he became welcoming of the restorying circles and opened up, sharing his own stories. The fact that he shared more difficult personal experiences over time within the restorying circles indicated this was a transformative practice.

The restorying circles allowed the participants to share experiences from their involvement within the criminal justice system and to reflect together on how to break free of this system. It gave them a sense of community, creating inspiration and pride as the men recognized their worth within the circle and their importance to the research that would potentially impact others down the road.

The restorying circles also demonstrated how negative past experiences (of family dysfunction, alcohol/drug abuse, violence, limited education, negative role modelling, loneliness, isolation, and criminal involvement) had propelled these participants toward involvement with the criminal justice system.

All shared how isolation acted as a shield against the violence and substance abuse that was often taking place within their family environments as children. The act of isolation in the beginning for many of these participants was out of necessity and self-preservation against the violence of their family members, who are supposed to love them and provide a sense of belonging. However, through self-isolation, the person no longer has others to provide support, nurture them, and offer guidance on life directions. What eventually happens is that this isolation seeps into this person's identity and begins to fester by speaking negative thoughts like "I'm not worthy of friends," "I don't deserve a family," and "I don't need support and love." Feelings like these often lead to negative behaviour such as drug/alcohol abuse, committing crime, and possibly suicide.

Ironically, the main purpose of the shield of isolation was initially to protect the child from violence often informed by substance abuse; however, these very same social factors later become manifest in the person's adolescent and adult lives as they commit acts of violence toward others and themselves, mostly under the influence of substances. Isolation, loneliness, and despair are all words that describe the participants' lives growing up as young people; these same words also describe the feelings of many who attempt suicide.

So many young people—especially Indigenous youth—feel alone, that nobody loves them, and that life isn't fair, leading to thoughts of suicide. These young people have often been forced into isolation by society and family dysfunction, and they use isolation as a shield for their protection; however, as time goes on, this shield increases their sense of abandonment, cutting them off from their families and communities.

Cut off from a circle of love and support. Many are left with only alcohol and drugs to numb their pain.

This isolation continued to be part of these participants' lives as they sought to escape with substance abuse as young adults and was exacerbated even further when they became incarcerated. Upon release, some participants realized that isolation and loneliness were no longer necessary and that seeking out cultural events and social gatherings was a better and healthier option. This change in their behaviour from isolation to community could be considered part of their restorying; the men now allowed new positive influences beyond their past negative experiences to shape their choices.

Reading the highlights of each participant's story allows us to understand how his life experiences influenced his eventual involvement with the criminal justice system. This isn't to say the participants were inevitably doomed to become offenders, but rather to recognize the commonalities among their life stories that rendered them more vulnerable to adverse involvement with the law. Hopefully, their examples will encourage others in similarly vulnerable positions to reshape, revise, and restory their stories, to assist them in avoiding pathways toward criminal involvement, and also inspire them to create safe spaces to share difficult experiences and the untold memories that may continue to limit and define them.

I hope this process will continue to benefit these men in the future; however, it's uncertain whether the six sessions of my PhD project were long enough to seriously impact the participants' future journeys. However, the question remains whether discussing other critical topics and issues would be worthwhile.

This study begs the question: are there ongoing spiritual and cultural supports and opportunities for building connections available to these participants and others with similar backgrounds and challenges now that our circles have concluded? Is there an ideal length of time for such gatherings, or should there be ongoing opportunities for restorying?

One of the valuable aspects of my PhD project was that the participants were committed and faithfully attended the circles. This helped to build a cohesive group and to increase trust and vulnerability within the circles. Perhaps if a different format were used, this connection would be lost, and the impact for each participant would be less significant. In other words, if the circles were ongoing in perpetuity, participants might not attend regularly, and the spirit of the community might be compromised.

Restorying circles offer a powerful avenue for healing and transformation, particularly those dealing with the complex interplay of past trauma and systemic injustice. My focus has been on incarcerated men and social services agencies, but this could easily translate as an approach for those working in education or health. By providing a safe, culturally grounded space for sharing stories, participants in restorying sessions confront their experiences, address the lingering effects of trauma, and forge new narratives for themselves. Ongoing supports and opportunities for connection beyond these sessions are essential to ensuring that the positive transformations achieved within the circles can be sustained over time.

The Medicine Wheel helps us understand things that we can't see physically but that include ideas or visions, teaching us to balance the emotional, mental, physical, and spiritual elements of our identities to stay healthy. Everyone who uses the Medicine Wheel will see things slightly differently. This difference is because everyone has their own unique gifts that are needed to serve themselves and others. Many cultures use different symbols for their own teachings of their stories. When we look into a Medicine Wheel, we see our weaknesses and our strengths. One must visualize oneself in the middle, connected to all points of the Medicine Wheel. The East is the place of new beginnings, and all of us will return to this place, as we experience new things in our lives. Everyone has a place in life's journey. If we do not or cannot recognize what we are to do in this journey, we tend not to grow as a person. Perhaps this is why many incarcerated Indigenous people have such difficulty understanding the nature of their journeys: due to their inability to recognize the gifts they were given at a young age. The most difficult and valuable gift of the South is to express one's feelings openly and freely and do so without hurting others. The gift of prayer occurs in the West. This allows us to be spiritually connected. People need to find room to pray to reflect on their creation and what they are to do with their lives. The greatest lesson of the West is to accept ourselves for who we really are. As human beings, we develop and grow in relation to our decisions, good and bad. Many people imagine themselves to have far less potential than they actually do. The North is the winter, white snow like the white hair of our Elders. Not all gifts come easy; gaining the wisdom of age takes hard work and patience. To be a whole person, according to the teachings of the Medicine Wheel, is to be alive in a physical, emotional, mental, and spiritual way.

Outro: Healing

> " *I am happy. Today, I am feeling more open, and I want more. I'm thinking about one-on-one talk. I'm sick and tired of hiding it. I want to feel better and more honest. I like this program because I got to learn more. It's important. I'm going forward to a better life. I keep working on it. Keep talking. I want more and more of the program.*"
> — Workshop Participant

If I could speak to my younger self now, I would tell him that I succeeded in my life in terms of having a decent job, raising a great family, marrying a beautiful lady, and having two awesome children, a boy and a girl. I would also tell my younger self that it wasn't his fault for all the mistakes that were made; it was just part of the journey. All the difficulties were meant to shape my life path the way it is. The old cliché: "things happen for a reason." But it all works out. I would make sure that my younger self heard this message loud and clear—that it did all work out for us.

Although the Indigenous men participating in my PhD project had undoubtedly experienced profound hardship throughout their lives—hardship implicated in their various pathways toward incarceration—each refused from the very beginning to have his narrative confined solely to negative personal history. The participants' narratives included not only their many experiences of abandonment, abuse, anger, despair, and self-destruction, but also experiences of learning from and caring for others, of cultural knowledge, and of personal strength and accomplishment. Although the men shared negative life experiences, which they often acknowledged as causally related to their eventual incarceration, threads of hope and resilience were woven throughout the stories.

Long-buried experiences of trauma lost some of their negative energy as they were shared in a supportive circle among others with similar stories. The men could not whisper words of worthlessness, despair, and self-destruction when all members of the group could see and recognize in their tales the efforts of a lonely and hurting child trying to survive in a largely uncaring environment. All research participants could witness each other's efforts toward self-preservation and protecting more vulnerable family members.

Listening to the stories of the other participants appeared to inspire each man to seek after threads of hope in his own story, to not only remember the painful moments, but indeed to recognize his own survival, strength, and resilience, to understand that even though past years seemed to "pass by in a haze," there could be a healthy future ahead.

Through restorying, I hope that Indigenous people gain a stronger sense of self-worth and self-identity and that they let go of the weight of past trauma that they cannot change. It is a tough task to ask someone not to let trauma affect them negatively, but it can be done. Restorying your story with the help of the Medicine Wheel Tipi model can empower people to reinterpret their past stories so they can live, feel, think, and act in a different way. It is not about reliving the past but learning from it. The same applies to restorying for non-Indigenous people. That is part of the reason I chose the MWT model—it includes all peoples in the circle. When you sit in a circle, it does not discriminate based on the colour of your skin or where you are from.

Canada can restory its story, too, creating a future that works for everyone. I believe that this new story would be one filled with kindness and respect. The Government of Canada would recognize and appreciate that Indigenous Peoples allowed them to live in and share this great country. It would honour First Nations, Métis, and Inuit people by treating them with authenticity and respect, living side-by-side and developing a healthy, friendly relationship. We would become brothers, sisters, and family to one another, since reciprocity was the spirit and intent of the treaties. The Government of Canada would treat Indigenous Peoples as they would want to be treated if the roles had been reversed and Indigenous Peoples had arrived in their overseas country.

Although it is exceedingly difficult to describe what that process would look like, I know what it would not look like.

There would be no residential schools, *Indian Act*, child welfare system, or colonial ideologies. Indigenous Peoples in what is now called Canada already had their way of living and were thriving. I encourage non-Indigenous people to reflect on how they can live with Indigenous Peoples in a respectful and harmonious manner, without disrupting their culture, way of life, or language. It is like someone is invited into your home. How would you act, and what would you do if you were an invited guest?

The Medicine Wheel Tipi Exercise

Now that you have read this book, you have an understanding of what can perpetuate the cycle of incarceration and abuse, and how people get stuck reliving their painful pasts. I've shown how restorying circles and the Medicine Wheel Tipi model can be used as part of a healing journey. I developed the following exercise as a starting point for readers to begin restorying their stories.

Before you begin, make sure you are in a comfortable environment where you feel safe. This exercise isn't so much about the solutions created; it is about trust, communication, perception and starting the journey of Restorying Your Story. The Medicine Wheel Tipi will act as a personally tailored tool that you can carry with you, which will continue to evolve as you continue to build on your healing journey.

It is important to note that this exercise can bring up intense and sometimes distressing emotions. Please make sure that you have a support system in place (friends, family, Elders, mental health professionals) that you can reach out to if you are feeling overwhelmed in any way. You can step away and come back to this at any time.

Preliminary questions to ask yourself

1. How has trauma impacted your life?
2. How has intergenerational trauma impacted your life?
3. Has poverty, addiction, and/or the foster care system impacted your life?
4. Did you experience a lack of resources and/or education?
5. Have you faced a lack of government support?
6. Did you grow up in a challenging or unsafe environment?
7. Have you been part of negative and/or toxic relationships?
8. *For Indigenous participants:* How have Residential Schools, the Child Welfare System, and Intergenerational Trauma impacted your life?

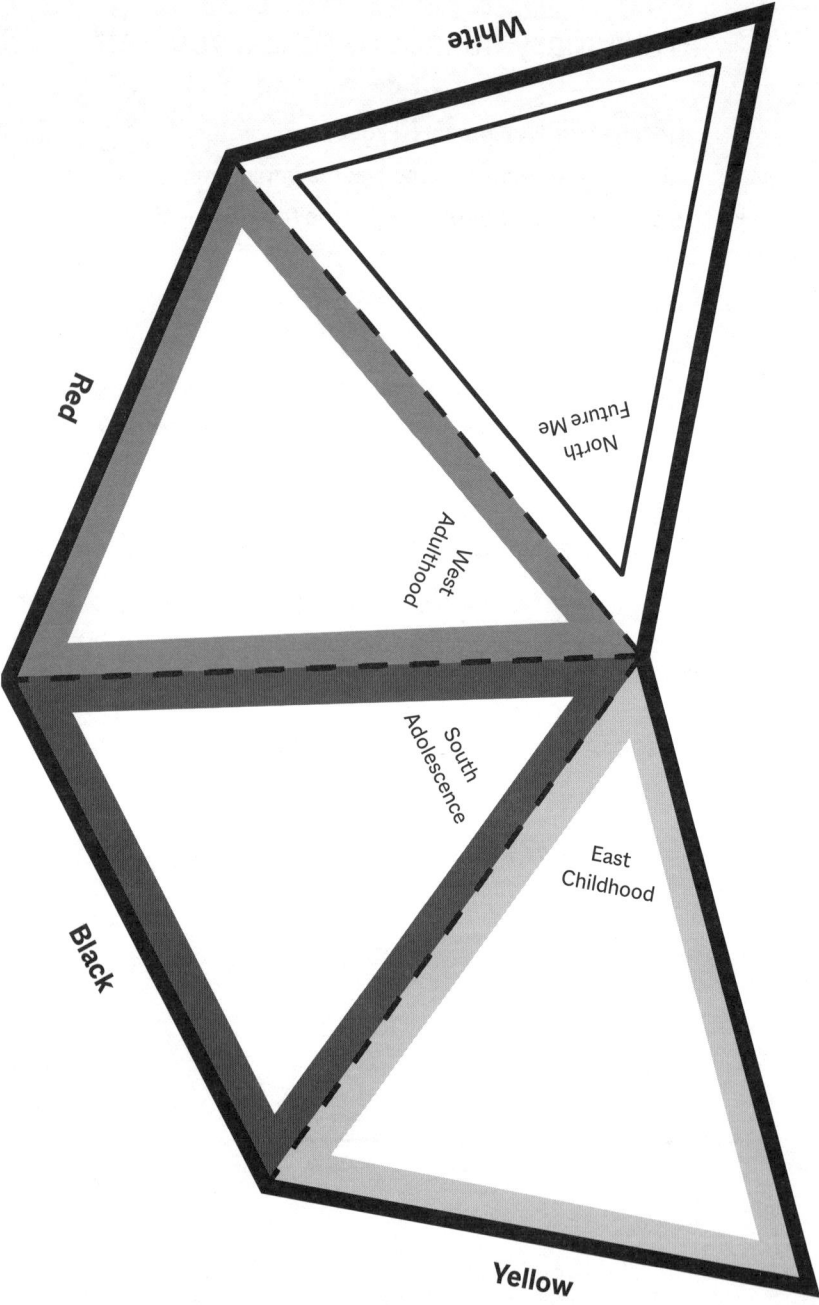

White

Red

North
Future Me

West
Adulthood

South
Adolescence

East
Childhood

Black

Yellow

The Medicine Wheel Tipi exercise

1. Make a copy of the Medicine Wheel Tipi image on the facing page.
2. Cut out the shape along the bold, black outline.
3. Fold along the dotted lines, turning your shape into 4 triangles to create your Tipi.
4. At the top of each coloured section, write the following titles:

    Yellow   East & Childhood

    Black   South & Adolescence

    Red   West & Adulthood

    White   North & Future Me
5. In each quadrant you will write keywords and phrases you associate with that part of your life.

I have provided some prompts, key words, and phrases, taken from previous restorying circles that you may find helpful as a starting point to describe your own experiences.

Tipi 1 Your Story

Quadrant 1 – East (Childhood)

Prompt: Describe your childhood—who raised you? Where did you live? Were you always with people? Were you lonely? Did you feel loved?

Key words

- unhealthy
- poverty
- hunger
- lack of parenting/role models
- lack of education
- family violence
- boredom
- isolation
- substance abuse
- residential school
- child welfare system (foster home, group home)
- cultural disconnection
- lack of identity

Phrases

- I felt dirty and awful
- I did not fit in
- I was left alone
- I was beaten up
- Family members left or passed away
- I rocked on the couch for hours to calm my nerves
- I don't know how to love or hug my kids
- I felt like no one loved me
- I did not want to live
- I was bullied
- People called me racist names

Quadrant 2 – South (Adolescence)

Prompt: Who were your role models? How were you treated by others? Was school a safe space for you? How did you cope with negative feelings?

Key words

- negative peers
- suicidal thoughts
- unkind words
- lack of trust
- tough on outside, weak on inside
- lack of emotions/feelings

Phrases

- I felt I had better chance of being sent to prison than graduating high school
- I am stupid and worthless
- I didn't care about my future because no one cared about me
- I never got a break in life
- I felt like a robot with no feelings or emotions
- I didn't know anything about my culture or ancestors
- I didn't know who I was
- I was lost

Quadrant 3 – West (Adulthood)

Prompt: What kinds of jobs have you had? Have you had a partner or children? Did you ever get in trouble with the law? Did you use drugs/alcohol? Have you experienced housing or food insecurity? What is your highest level of education? Do you have a good support system?

Key words

- Past mistakes
- Change of heart
- Disrespect toward self and others
- Violence
- No friends
- Ongoing addiction
- Feeling stuck
- Toxic relationships
- Abuse

Phrases

- I know I need help, I just don't know how to ask
- I have learned from my mistakes and I have a change of heart
- I need to be there for my kids
- I treat people like they treat me most times
- I am not attractive to others or myself
- I am trapped in a lose/lose situation
- I suffer in silence
- I have difficulty connecting with others
- I don't trust anyone
- I'm repeating cycles of abuse
- I am always anticipating fight
- I hurt myself
- I have no tools to deal with relationships in a positive way
- I don't know how to express emotions
- I used to love drugs/alcohol
- I am addicted to spirituality

Quadrant 4 – North (Future Me)

Prompt: Do you have hope for your future? Can you envision a future for yourself? What goals are you working toward? Have you experienced any cultural and/or spiritual activities?

Key words

- Spirituality
- Relationships
- My children
- Low self esteem
- No opportunities
- Shame

Phrases

- I dropped out of college
- I hate my job
- When things get tough I give up
- I'm afraid to reach out to cultural leaders
- I don't like who I am
- I keep relapsing
- I can't see a good future for myself and my family
- I have a hard time sharing my experiences with others
- I am afraid I won't be able to provide for my new baby
- I don't trust myself

After you've completed your first tipi, take time to reflect on the many twists and turns that have taken the innocent and healthy life you were given at birth and brought you to where you are today. Tipi 1 helps you identify that you were not provided with the right conditions you needed to thrive. Your past is part of you, but it doesn't define you; you can reconstruct it to make different choices moving forward.

At this point in a restorying circle, we would often have an Elder smudge to release the negative energy to start the path to a healthier place. I encourage readers to release any negative energy and emotions that come up during the first half of this exercise. You can light a candle or incense, smudge, meditate, or take a walk as a way of diffusing the negative energy.

At this part of the process, you are asked to take Tipi 1 and turn it inside out, creating Tipi 2. Symbolically, the unhealthy past is now overtaken by the healthy present and future.

Tipi 2
Restorying Your Story

The fabric of our lives includes strong and weak threads. Now we revisit the directions of the MWT and bring forward your strengths and gifts in the different parts of your journey. We need to learn how to use the past and future to weave a strong personal fabric to help us move forward.

You will now repeat the previous exercise with a new healthier focus on Tipi 2, by creating positive words for each quadrant. This starts the healthy review of where you are going. It doesn't have to be large steps; small steps of healthy decisions and outlook are a more realistic approach.

Remember to affirm your unique gifts, strengths, and worth. Visualize new and more hopeful outcomes of challenges in your life.

Quadrant 1 - East (Childhood)

Prompt: What positive memories do you have of your childhood? Who loved you? What was your favourite place?

Key words

- Sisters
- Sports
- Favourite snack
- Summers with Grandpa
- Learning from the land

Phrases

- My sister always tucked me in at night
- I made a friend at summer camp
- Grandpa taught me how to hunt
- I learned first-aid
- I discovered a love of reading at the library

Quadrant 2 - South (Adolescence)

Prompt: What positive memories do you have of your teen years? Who helped you survive? Who did you help? Did you have dreams or goals? Where/When were you the happiest? Who were your role models? How were you treated by others? Was school a safe space for you? How did you cope with negative feelings?

Key words

- Safe place
- Kind words
- Good friend
- Let my guard down
- Sports as outlet
- Talented at art
- My first love
- Laughed with siblings

Phrases

- Mr. Doe let me eat lunch in his classroom when other students were bullying me
- I fed my siblings with my hunting skills
- I taught my brother to read
- I got a summer job at the fair
- I made my friend feel better when her parents got divorced
- My sister could depend on me

Quadrant 3 – West (Adulthood)

Prompt: What lessons are you learning? How have you survived? What are your gifts and abilities? Has anyone told you that you are good at something? Do you have children? How have you cared for your children?

Key words

- Hunting and being on the land
- Sweat Lodge ceremonies
- Exercise
- Getting enough to eat
- Friends
- Safety
- Family
- Found-family

Phrases

- I asked my cousin for help
- I got my High School Diploma
- I went to rehab
- My kids can rely on me
- I left my abusive ex
- I have learned from my mistakes
- I am learning to take responsibility for my actions
- I treat people with respect

Quadrant 4 – North (Future Me)

Prompt: Do you have hope for your future? Can you envision a future for yourself? What goals are you working toward? Have you experienced any cultural and/or spiritual activities? What teachings are important to learn and include in your life? What talents would you like to develop? Who could help you on your journey? Who could you help?

Key words:

- Healing
- Spirituality
- My family
- Self esteem
- New opportunities
- Pride
- Community

Phrases:

- I'm going back to school
- I am good at my new job
- When things get tough I pray
- Spiritual ceremonies are powerful tools for healing
- I like who I am
- I relapsed, but I went back to rehab
- I can see a good future for myself and my family
- I share my experiences with youth so they can make better choices
- I am on my sobriety journey
- I would do anything for my new baby
- I am learning to trust myself
- I'm teaching myself how to paint

Conclusion: Moving Toward a Healthier Future

Acknowledging that we all start with a pure, clean slate which is then altered due to circumstances we are often not in control of, forms who we have become (Tipi 1). Coming to terms with these moments of pain is important in creating a pathway forward.

However, we need to ensure we don't dwell on them and instead turn our focus on who we want to be in a new healthier direction (Tipi 2). This results in us knowing we can write our new story, Restory our Story.

You now have two Tipis which you can continue to use as a reference for the future. More specifically you can continue to grow your second Tipi by setting new goals and making incremental positive changes in your life.

After completing the Tipi exercise, please take care of yourself. You have completed a major first step in your restorying journey. Thank you for engaging with this exercise and making moves toward a healthier future.

References

Archibald, J. (2008). *Indigenous storywork: Educating the heart, mind, body, and spirit*. Vancouver, B.C: UBC Press.

Bishop, R. (1999). *Collaborative Storytelling: Meeting Indigenous Peoples' Desires for Self-Determination in Research*. Paper presented at the World Indigenous People's Conference, Albuquerque, New Mexico, June 15-22.

Brown, L. A., & Strega, S. (2005). *Research as resistance: Critical, Indigenous and anti-oppressive approaches*. Canadian Scholars' Press.

Corntassel, J. (2009). Indigenous storytelling, truth-telling, and community approaches to reconciliation. *ESC: English Studies in Canada, 35*(1), 137–159.

Dauvergne, M. (2012). *Adult correctional statistics in Canada*, 2010/2011.

Dion, S. D. (2009). *Braiding histories: Learning from Aboriginal peoples' experiences and perspectives*. UBC Press.

Gauthier, M. (2010). *The impact of the residential school, child welfare system and intergenerational trauma upon the incarceration of Aboriginals* [Master's thesis, Queen's University]. https://qspace.library .queensu.ca/server/api/core/bitstreams/fc803708 -d65e-43ce-90df-8ad5acb24ce5/content.

Gauthier, M. (2017). *Restorying the lives of Aboriginal People connected with the criminal justice system* [Doctorial dissertation, Queen's University]. http://hdl.handle.net/1974/22610.

Haney, C. (2001). *The psychological impact of incarceration: Implications for post-prison adjustment.* Retrieved on November 15, 2016; from http://aspe.hhs.gov/hsp/prison2home02/Haney.htm.

Howell, T. (2008). *The point of no return: Aboriginal offenders' journey towards a crime free life* [Doctoral dissertation, University of British Columbia].

Hyatt, A. E. (2013). Healing through culture for incarcerated Aboriginal people. *First Peoples Child & Family Review, 8*(2), 40-53.

Karp, D. (2010). Unlocking men, unmasking masculinities: Doing men's work in Prison. *Journal of Men's Studies, 18*(1), 63-83.

Kings County Advertiser. *Conditions Imposed.* Retrieved on January 27th, 2017; from http://www.kingscountynews.ca/news/local/2016/10/16/parole-board-imposes-specialconditions-4664598.html.

Krech, P. R. (2002). Envisioning a healthy future: A re-becoming of Native American men. *Journal of Society & Social Welfare, 29(1),* 77-95.

LaForme, H. S. (2005). "Justice System in Canada: Does It Work for Aboriginal People?" *Indigenous Law Journal, 4,* 1.

Latimer, J., & Foss, L. C. (2004). A One-Day Snapshot of Aboriginal Youth in Custody across Canada: Phase II. *Ottawa, ON: Research and Statistics Division, Department of Justice Canada.* https://www.justice.gc.ca/eng/rp-pr/cj-jp/yj-jj/yj2-jj2/yj2.pdf.

Lavallee, L.F. (2009). Practical application of an Indigenous research framework and the qualitative Indigenous research methods: Sharing circles and Anishnaabe symbol-based reflection. *International Journal of Qualitative Methods, 8*(1), 21–40.

Linden, R. (2001). *Crime prevention in Aboriginal communities.* University of Manitoba. http://www.ajic.mb.ca/crime.pdf.

Maruna, S. (1999, March). Desistance and development: The psychosocial process of going straight. *The British Criminology Conferences: Selected Proceedings* (Vol. 2).

Matsakis, A. (1998). *Trust after trauma: A guide to relationships for survivors and those who love them.* New Harbinger Publications, Inc.

McCormick, R. (1994). The facilitation of healing for the First Nations people of British Columbia. *Canadian Journal of Native Education, 21*(2), 251–322.

McKegney, S. (2007). *Magic weapons: Aboriginal writers remaking community after residential school.* University of Manitoba Press.

McKegney, S (Ed). (2014). *Masculindians: Conversations about Indigenous manhood.* University of Manitoba Press.

Meseyton, H. R. (2005). *Daughters of Indian residential school survivors* [Doctoral dissertation, University of British Columbia].

Milloy, J. (1999). *A national crime.* Winnipeg, Manitoba: University of Manitoba Press.

McVie, F. (2001). *Drugs in federal corrections—The issues and challenges.* Retrieved on December 11, 2016; from https://publications.gc.ca/collections/collection_2024 /scc-csc/JS83-2-13-3-eng.pdf

Nielsen, M. O. (2003). Canadian Aboriginal healing lodges: A model for the United States? *The Prison Journal, 83*(1), 67–89.

Psychalive. (2016). "Psychology for everyday." Retrieved on December 7, 2016; from http://www.psychalive.org /isolation-and-loneliness.

Royal Commission on Aboriginal Peoples. (1996). *Final Report.* Government of Canada.

Rosenthal, G. (2003). The healing effects of storytelling: On the conditions of curative storytelling in the context of research and counseling. *Qualitative Inquiry, 9*(6), 915933.

Rudin, J. (2005). *Aboriginal peoples and the criminal justice system.* (pp. 1-73). Ipperwash Inquiry.

Rymhs, D. (2008). *From the iron house: Imprisonment in First Nations writing (Vol. 8).* Wilfrid Laurier University Press.

Sabo, D. F., Kupers, T. A., & London, W. (Eds.). (2001). *Prison masculinities.* Philadelphia: Temple University Press.

Smith, Linda Tuhuwai. (2012). *Decolonizing methodologies: Research and Indigenous peoples.* Zed Books.

SPIRIT MATTERS: Aboriginal People and the Corrections and Conditional Release Act. Retrieved on March 3, 2017; from *www.thestarphoenix.com/... /aboriginal_people_and_the_corrections_and_conditional*

Thibodeau, S., & Peigan, F. N. (2007). Loss of trust among First Nation people: Implications when implementing child protection treatment initiatives. *First Peoples Child & Family Review, 3*(4), 50–58.

Tousignant, M., & Sioui, N. (2009). Resilience and Aboriginal communities in crisis: Theory and interventions. *International Journal of Indigenous Health, 5*(1), 43–61.

Truth and Reconciliation Commission of Canada. (2016). *Honouring the truth, reconciling for the future: Summary of the Final Report of the Truth and Reconciliation Commission of Canada.* (Government of Canada)

Vaillant, G. E. (1993). *The wisdom of the ego.* Harvard University Press.

Voyageur, C. J., Brearley, L., & Calliou, B. (Eds.). (2014). *Restorying Indigenous leadership: Wise practices in community development.* Banff Centre Press.

Wagamese, Richard. (2017). *Richard Wagamese > Quotes > Quotable Quote.* Goodreads. Retrieved on January 29, 2017; from http://www.goodreads.com/quotes/757371-all-that-we-are-is-story-from-the-moment-we

Waldram, J. (1997). The Aboriginal people of Canada: Colonial and mental health. *Ethnicity, immigration, and psychopathology.* New York: Plenum Press.

Waldrum, J. B. (1997). *The way of the pipe: Aboriginal spirituality and the symbolic healing in Canadian prisons.* Broadview Press.

Welsh, A., & Ogloff, J. (2008). An empirical evaluation of the judicial consideration of Aboriginal status in sentencing decisions. *Canadian Journal of Criminology and Criminal Justice, 50*(4), 491–517.

Wesley-Esquimaux, C., & Calliou, B. (2010). Best practices in Aboriginal community development: A literature review and wise practices approach. *The Banff Centre.*

Wilson, G. (2002). *Working together: Enhancing the role of Aboriginal communities in Federal corrections.* Correctional Service of Canada. Retrieved December 05, 2016; from http://www.csc- scc.gc.ca/aboriginal/002003 -3003-eng.shtml

Winnicott, D. W. (1965). *The maturational processes and the facilitating environment: Studies in the theory of emotional development.* M. M. R. Khan (Ed.). London: Hogarth Press.

Woolner, C. (March 2009). Re-storying Canada's past: A case study in the significance of narratives in healing intractable conflict. University of Notre Dame. Retrieved December 6, 2016; https://www.beyondintractability.org /casestudy/woolner-re-storying

York, G. (1990). *The dispossessed: Life and death in native Canada.* Random House (UK).

About the Author

Dr. Michael Gauthier is a survivor of the trauma caused by the residential school program. He has translated these negative life experiences into an inspirational self-development philosophy and education program. Michael advocates for those who are struggling with their past trauma through his and his business partner's company, Life-Circle.

He graduated from Queen's University with both a PhD in Cultural Studies and a Masters degree in Education. Holding consultative and functional positions within the criminal justice system has allowed him the privilege to work as a negotiator, police officer, correctional officer, Indigenous Community Development officer, and a parole officer over the past three decades. Michael is the father of two children, and has been married to his wife Carolyn for 25 years. Michael's First Nation community is Taykwa Tagamou, a Cree community located in Northern Ontario.